EMPLOYEE RELATIONSHIP
MANAGEMENT

MJP
PUBLISHERS

EMPLOYEE RELATIONSHIP MANAGEMENT

Dr. V. Chitra

Assistant Professor,
Department of Commerce,
Kristu Jayanti College (Automonous),
K Narayanapura, Konnathur P.O, Bangalore.

Dr. R. Shanthi

Assistant Professor,
Department of Commerce,
University of Madras, Chennai - 600 005

MJP
PUBLISHERS

Chennai   New Delhi   Tirunelveli

MJP
PUBLISHERS

ISBN 978-81-8094-355-3 **MJP Publishers**

All rights reserved · No. 44, Nallathambi Street,
Printed and bound in India · Triplicane, Chennai 600 005

MJP 261 · © Publishers, 2017

Publisher : **C. Janarthanan**

Project Editor : **C. Ambica**

This book has been published in good faith that the work of the author is original. All efforts have been taken to make the material error-free. However, the author and publisher disclaim responsibility for any inadvertent errors.

I dedicate this work to my family with a special feeling of gratitude to my loving parents, Srinivasan & Susila Srinivasan and to my husband Pradeep Venkatachari whose words of encouragement pushed me up to write this book. My sisters and Brothers have never left my side and are very special. I also dedicate this book to all my friends and colleague who have supported me throughout the process. I will always appreciate all they have done.

ACKNOWLEDGEMENT

At the outset, I thank my parents and almighty with whose blessings it was possible to complete this book successfully.

I would like to express my gratitude to all those who provided support, talked things over, read, wrote, offered comments, allowed me to quote their remarks and assisted in the editing, proofreading and design.

I would like to thank my philosopher and guide Dr. R. Shanthi for enabling me to publish this book. Above all I want to thank my Mom, Dad, Brothers, Sisters and Husband, who supported and encouraged me in spite of all the time that took me away from them. It was a long and difficult journey for them.

I would like to extend my gratitude to Rev.Fr. Josekutty P.D, Principal, Rev. Fr. Augustine George, Vice principal Dean and Head of the departments and my colleagues, Kristu Jayanti College (Autonomous), Bangalore -77 for their constant support.

I would like to thank MJP Publishers for helping me in the process of selection and editing. Thanks to Mr.Jana, my publisher who encouraged me in this regard.

Last, but not least, I beg forgiveness of all those who have been with me over the course of the years and whose names I have failed to mention. I thank them the most. I thank one and all who have helped me in every little way in achieving what seemed a task too very big successfully with ease.

PREFACE

This book presents research-based best practices related to Employee Relationship Management and offers content area strategies that integrate employer- employee relationship in an organization. These strategies are based on the theory of organization and theory of equilibrium, which can be applied in every organization, no matter regarding the level of employment. Various research scales to measure Employee relationship management and suggestions for improving the relationship are included in this book. Following are the Chapters included in this book. The brief summary of these chapters are listed below.

Chapter — 1

This chapter is a prolog to employee-employer relationship. The author explained key components of ERM based on Social-exchange theory, power-inducement theory, contribution and equilibrium theory. In addition to this, the author clearly stated the importance, objective and purpose of the study. Based on the purpose (i.e., to bring out the relationship between ERM dimensions, individual well-being and their work place behavior) research problem and questions were formulated. To obtain answers to research questions the detailed investigation were done; this study is descriptive in nature, concentrates only on managers and employees working in leading public sector banks operating in Chennai. Based on the pilot study the questionnaire was modified and main study was conducted. Purposive sampling was adopted to collect the data. The mean and standard deviation determined through pilot study in turn was used to determine the sample size for this study. Through this calculation the sample size for Employee was arrived as 243 and sample size for manager was arrived as 115. Normality test, Reliability analysis, Frequency analysis, ANOVA, Independent t test, Factor analysis, Regression analysis, Discriminant analysis, SEM analysis were performed to prove the hypotheses followed by pilot study report and Limitations of the study.

Chapter - **2**

Summarizing the results of chapter – 2, it can be stated that ERM dimensions have indeed a positive effect on individual well-being and their work place behavior. The review about research on employee relationship management and their relationship towards the individual well-being and individual work place behavior, existing studies that controlled for ERM dimensions such as psychological contract, empowerment, employee involvement, cultural intelligence, organisational support, psychological ownership and inrole performance also found significant relationship between ERM variables and Individual well-being and OCB.

Based on the review of literature it is established that the psychological contract, Cultural intelligence, psychological ownership has a positive effect on individual work place behavior. Psychological empowerment showed positive effects on Individual well-being i.e., psychological well-being and organisational commitment. Employee involvement, perceived organisational support and in-role performance positively impact both individual well-being and their work place behavior. The review on relationship between job attitudes, individual well-being and their workplace behavior revealed that it is mostly mediated by the in-role performance.

Though there is sufficient research evidence of relationship between variables and many studies have shown the importance of individual well-being and work outcomes, only few systematic studies have provided empirical evidence of relationship between employer-employee relationship towards individual well-being and individual work place behavior. Most of the studies have concentrated on psychological contract or psychological empowerment or employee involvement or cultural intelligence or psychological ownership or perceived organisational support or in-role performance separately towards individual well-being or individual work place behavior and not extended in measuring the effects of all the above-mentioned variables towards individual well-being and their work place behavior.

In the light of the above discussion this study aims to fill the research gap by measuring comprehensive set of ERM dimensions towards individual well-being and individual work place behavior from both employees and managers perception.

Chapter – 3

Most of the research focused mainly on performance and well-being of employee in an organisation. This research is diversified to explore the relationship between Managers and Employees perception regarding ERM factors towards employee well being, their level of commitment and also their behavior at work place. Based on the above discussion the conceptual model was developed to understand the various factors influencing public sector bank employee and managers relationship. This model helps both manager and employees to understand each other's perception. Summarizing the results it is identified that ERM dimensions have positive effect on individual well-being and their work place behavior. The main purpose of this study was to examine the relationship between comprehensive set of ERM variables towards individual wellbeing and their work place behavior. The framework enlighten that ERM has a positive impact on the psychological wellbeing, organisational commitment and organizational citizenship behavior.

Chapter – 4

This chapter provides the analytical details and discussion of the study by using SPSS and AMOS. Further this book is used to know the appropriate techniques to measure employees in the organization

Chapter – 5

This chapter provides a brief summary of findings, suggestion – to employees, to managers and to management in order to improve the employee-employer relationship.

In conclusion

Every employee in an organisation spends maximum time at their workplace; therefore it is more than imperative to treat them as a part of extended family. A small initiative that is more associated to fun and celebration can go a long way in building better employee engagement that results in better commitment. Strong employment relation helps employees to maintain good work culture and good work environment. Culture makes the employees emotionally attached towards the organisation.

ABBREVIATIONS

DV   Dependent Variable

EE   Employee

EI   Employee Involvement

ER   Employer

EOR   Employee Organization Relationship

ERM   Employee Relationship Management

IV   Independent Variable

IRP   In Role Performance

OC   Organizational Commitment

OCB   Organizational Citizenship Behavior

PC   Psychological Contract

PE   Psychological Empowerment

PO   Psychological Ownership

PW   Psychological Well-Being

PDM   Participation In Decision Making

POS   Perceived Organizational Support

PSM   Public Service Motivation

LIST OF TABLES

LIST OF FIGURES

CONTENTS

1

INTRODUCTION

1.1 INTRODUCTION TO EMPLOYEE RELATIONSHIP MANAGEMENT (ERM)

Employee relationship management is an ability to manage the relationship between employees working in the same team or from different teams. Employee Relationship Management is an activity that helps to increase the relationship among the employees through which everyone is satisfied by the strong association with each other. The importance of the individual in an organisation may be understood in many ways. Like two sides in a coin, in which his capabilities, conviction and concentration are considered as employees positive side. Whereas, in negative side his absence of delusion, vanity and immaturity are the basic requirements that make individual an effective employee and by managing such employees in turn makes good organisation.

Employees are considered to be an unbeatable energy and source of every organisation but the right way of simulation will help to yield progress, which starts with good relationship. Employee–employer relationship is an unwritten mutual contract between the employer and employee. Here Managers act as an agent of employers having authority to take decision and employees have to follow it. Both Employee–employer relations and employee–organisation relationships were considered as an important factor for the organisation's internal relationship management.

Based on the Social Exchange, Inducement-contribution, Power Dependency, Role and Equilibrium theory the following components are found to play a key role in healthy employer–employee relationship.

Communication

Communication is one of the important factors that shape employer–employee relationship. Any form of communication be it visual, verbal or through action does play a vital role in garnering better clarity of anything that is done or to be done within or outside an organisation. An organisation is deemed healthy only when it is able to clearly communicate its objectives in a manner that is understood by one and all in a proper manner. Through effective communication an organisation has reaped greater benefits than the ones that have not given a thought to this aspect of management. Communication is an organisational wide initiative that has to be practiced continuously. Communication therefore can never cease to exist, which is the key reason for the soundness of organisation.

Promoting Team Activities at the Workplace

Motivating the employees to work together as a team in an organisation should improve ways and means in order to promote a team culture. Gone are the days when individuals made the difference. The new era calls for people who are willing to be a part of the team and share success rather than to be focused on self. The thought that nobody is indispensible is the theory behind a team culture. After all two is better than one. This only boosts energy, encourages healthy discussion, improves confidence, builds trust and promotes knowledge sharing.

Commitment

Commitment is a psychosomatic feel that connect an individual to the organisation. It refers to the possibility of an individual staying connected with the organisation for a long time, feel emotionally attached to it, irrespective of the fact whether the job is satisfying or challenging or not. Companies often feel that retention and commitment are interchangeable theories. It would be incorrect to assume that an employee who has been long serving in the company would be committed. Highly profitable and performing companies do realize that employee commitment is one of the major factors that drive success.

Empowerment

Getting employee to own their task and perform is one of the most challenging attribute for an organisation. A forward thinking organisation often encourages its team members to take calculated risk, learn from mistakes and make appropriate decisions without any wrong assumptions. This approach is commonly referred as an empowerment. Through this strong tool employees make decisions within their span. Employee empowerment provides great mobility for the employees to love what they do, keeps them highly motivated to contribute for the organisation and betterment of self. This not only improves internal health but also drives better customer interaction and experience.

Well-being

A study by Elton Mayo around right illumination and how it influences better workplace was a major breakthrough and provided enough steam for organisation to take workplace well-being very seriously. Workplace well being is an approach to create a good working environment in order to have its employees better engagement. Right place, right people, right infrastructure and right benefits would attract great commitment from employees and thrusts to go above and beyond.

Involvement

Employee involvement basically depends on the work atmosphere in which people feel empowered to make decisions which not only affects the organisation but also their job. This is usually spoken in a positive sense as it provides a great push for the employees to work better and feel passionate about what and how they are going to do their jobs. Employee involvement is a leadership philosophy through which employees are enabled to contribute towards betterment of the organisation. Every employee should be treated with respect and not just as a human being. Every contribution must be treated and appreciated as something that would help to achieve its goals and no bias or prejudice should be entertained or encouraged. Under this philosophy employees in the business are involved in taking the organisation forward.

1.2   NEED AND IMPORTANCE OF ERM

Nowadays, every organisation practices human resource management where they plan and allocate resources as per the organisation requirement. Human resource is pervasive in nature, where every employee in the organisation must add flavor to the taste of success through his/her participation. Employee's participation is possible by the way of team work which leads to the good understanding among the employees through which they get strongly bounded with the connection as in the name of "Employee Relations". Every second has exposed to some great inventions and a great world in our hand as we move. In that sense starting and ending point of any invention is by a human. Organisations are quick to adopt any changes in advance technologies and quick to embrace the same. As much for their technology and change in the dependency something that hasn't changed in history of time is the innate dependency on people. This therefore is probably the most critical aspect for any organisation. The success and progress of any organisation sticks on how employees and managers move in their work place.

Several researches have been carried out to understand the Employer–Employee relationship. Every employee/employer in an organisation has certain relationship between them so as to make work environment peaceful. Employment relations make managers and employees get into the psychological contract which helps to build the transitional, transactional and transformational relationship. This type of relationship helps the employee to behave positively in an organisation by which they support each other. Sharing, giving guidelines to peers about their work related issues by joining their hands to work for the welfare and betterment of the organisation. Work environment plays a vital role in employee satisfaction which makes employees to be committed and empowered. Empowered employee can achieve more when given the room to own what they do. Maintaining the healthy employee relationship is very important for a successful organisation.

Employee's wellbeing facilitates to maintain a strong interpersonal relationship among employees and rally around job satisfaction, life satisfaction and happiness thereby reducing the unnecessary tension and stress. Healthy relationship reduces the conflict among employees and also makes them to feel as though they belong to the same family. This is essential for a team work. Team work and inclusive culture can help the organisation to resolve issues. Good relationship between managers/employees helps in building loyalty and trust and thereby driving customer satisfaction. Strong relationship among manager and employee provides a positive thought about the work place and friendly approach between them helps in building the progressive organisation.

This book is an attempt to provide the subjective experience of the employment relationship from various frames of reference viz. organisational citizenship behavior, psychological ownership, in-role performance and psychological contract in order to explain the individual-level explanations to link between manager and employee and also further helps the manager to understand the employee obligation and expectations towards their employment.

This book aims to highlight the relationship between well-being, empowerment, perceived organisational support, psychological contract, commitment and involvement for both manager and employee and also helps in understanding the need for a healthy and less stressful workforce which in turn contribute to the improved mental and physical health as well as job satisfaction.

1.3 AIM OF THE BOOK

Based on the above discussion the following objectives were identified.

Primary objectives

- To explore the ERM factors on individual well-being and their work place behavior.

- To determine factors influencing Employee relationship management.

- To find out the relationship between ERM dimensions and psychological wellbeing, OC and OCB.

- To propose a model on ERM dimensions and psychological well-being, organisational commitment and organisational citizenship behavior.

Secondary objectives

- To identify the differences between employee and manager by applying ERM dimensions.

- To identify the differences between employee and managers based on psychological well-being, Organisational commitment and organisational citizenship behavior.

- To evaluate managers and employees perception towards ERM dimensions and psychological well-being, Organisational commitment and Organisational citizenship behavior based on their personal characteristics.

- To find out the association between job satisfaction and happiness of employees and managers working in the public sector bank.

- To analyze the significant difference between age group and friendly relationship of employees and managers working in the public sector bank.

The birth of Liberalization, Privatization and Globalization (LPG) and foreign policies has generated many positive impacts in employer-employee relationship. The footprint of the concept of employer-employee relationship is seen in the corporate like IT, ITES, BPO and private financial services and also rapid emerge of turnover intention and lack of staffing leads to analysis of Employer-Employee relationship and its impact on psychological well-being, organisational commitment and organisational citizenship behavior of employee/managers working in the public sector banks.

There is a general sense of belief that a secure job offers great working culture. This belief is true in public sector banks as well. The public sector bank administration believes that by providing a secured job to the employees, the relationship will not be tarnished. In reality employees seem unhappy with the managerial relationship and have cited many problem areas such as long working hours, inadequate support and more work pressure. It is essential to find out effect of ERM characteristics such as psychological contract, psychological empowerment, employee involvement, cultural intelligence, perceived organisational support, psychological ownership and inrole performance on psychological well-being, organisational commitment and organisational citizenship behavior in the banks. In recent times public sector banks are facing employee turnover issue and need to manage diverse work culture; hence an understanding of the relationship of ERM and its outcome in this sector is required.

Therefore the main purpose of this book is to understand the ERM factors and examine reasons for their impact on employees/managers well-being towards their behavior in banks. This book brings about a focus on employment relationship between managers and employees and provide recommendations to improve the employee employer relationship and experience.

This book aims to bring out the relationship between ERM dimensions, individual well being and their work place behavior.

1.4 TECHNIQUES USED FOR ANALYSIS

Various research scales to measure Employee relationship management and suggestions for improving the relationship are included in the book. SPSS and AMOS version 16 were used to analyze the data collected from the study. The following techniques were used.

- Normality test has been used to test the sample adequacy.

- Reliability analysis was used to know the repeatability and accuracy of the data. Frequency analysis has been used to measure the personal and organisational details.

- ANOVA analysis was done to know the significant difference between more than two groups.

- Independent sample't' test was performed to know the mean differences between two groups.

- Factor analysis was used to find the predominant factor influencing the Employer–Employee relationship among public sector bank managers and employees.

- Regression analysis was used to find out the relationship between dependent and independent variable.

- Discriminant analysis was used to find the correct classification proportion of the sample data.

- Structural equation modelling was used to fit a model and also to explain the relationship between dependent variable and independent variable.

1.5   CHAPTER ARRANGEMENTS

The book comprises five chapters that deal with the author's research on Employee relationship management.

Chapter 1: Introduction

The chapter aims at explaining the need and importance of the study on ERM, the objective of the study, methodology and the limitations of the study.

Chapter 2: Dimensions of ERM

This chapter includes literature related to the dimensions of psychological contract, psychological empowerment, employee involvement, cultural intelligence, organisational support, psychological ownership, inrole performance, psychological well-being, organisational commitment and organisational citizenship behavior. These were drawn from books and journals. Based on these literatures the theoretical framework and hypotheses are developed.

Chapter 3: ERM Theories

The chapter discusses the Theories and provides a theoretical model.

Chapter 4: Analytical Details and Discussions on ERM

This chapter is concerned with the result of statistical analysis. To get appropriate result SPSS was used to analyze the data.

Chapter 5: Findings and Conclusions

This chapter summarizes research findings, suggestions and conclusion drawn from the research conducted by the author.

REFERENCES

This includes in alphabetical order the list of related books, academic journal, working paper series and all past dissertation used in the research.

DIMENSIONS OF ERM

2.1 INTRODUCTION

This chapter includes previous research studies related to the dimensions of ERM such as psychological contract, psychological empowerment, employee involvement, cultural intelligence, organisational support, psychological ownership, in-role performance, psychological well-being, organisational commitment and organisational citizenship behavior from both managers and employee's perspective, which they experience in their work place.

2.2 PSYCHOLOGICAL CONTRACT

This section of the chapter deals with researches on psychological contract in the organisational context and considers organisation as a social system.

Shore and Tetrick (1994) theoretically investigated the role of psychological contract in organisations. Further this study examined the meaning and functions of the psychological contract including factors that contribute to its formation. Based on the earlier research, they finally concluded that the psychological contract is an important organisational phenomenon which provides a basis for understanding the link between employee and their organisations, they clarify the nature of psychological contract breach, violation, perceptual and cognitive processes by which each developed their employment relationship.

Roehling, Cavanaugh, Moynihan and Boswell (1998) seeks to provide information and guidance to HR professionals regarding the new employment relationship. Further, this study investigated the extent to which there is a consensus in the literature regarding the changes in employment relations. For investigation purpose 51 articles were selected from 800 business related publications in order to examine the content coding and to analyze articles regarding the new employment relationship. Results proved that for every successful management, new employment relationship will be required. Further, human resource professionals have to execute their role effectively.

Millward and Brewerton (1999) examined the contractor emotional attachment towards their organisation by assuming that contractors are highly estimative, influential towards their organisational interest and emotional investment, and further explored the relationship between contractors psychological contract, social attraction, team spirit and intention to leave. For this purpose a study was conducted among 62 permanent agency contractor and 55 temporary agency contractors and 86 fixed term contract employees were taken. The results showed that there is a significant differences between contractors and employees emotional investment towards their organisation. In case of transactional and exchange consideration contractors were highly significant than that of their employee, but this result did not stop the development of relational relationship between the contractors and employee. Further this study also found that the relational contracts were mainly predicted by team spirit and organisational identification.

Coyle-Shapiro and Kessler (2000) examined manager and employee's perception of psychological contract and its impact towards the organisational commitment and organisational behavior. For this purpose they conducted the survey among managers and employee working in public service sector. Public service includes educational institutions, health sector and social care. The study results proved that the majority of employees were not satisfied with employment relations towards their manager, the same was felt by the manager towards their employees. Further research finalizes that in order to equalize the employment relations with their manager, employees reduce their commitment and also enthusiasm to engage in OCB·

Guest and Conway (2002) have predominantly focused only on employee perceptions of the psychological contract. This article begins to level out the balance by reporting a study, based on a survey of 1,306 senior HR managers that explores the management of the psychological contract and in particular the role of organisational communication. Three distinct and relevant aspects of organisational communication are identified and they are concerned with initial entry, day to day work and more future oriented, top-down communication. Effectual use of these forms of communication is associated with what manager's judge to be a clearer and less frequently breached set of organisational promises and commitments.

While a fairer exchange and a more positive impact of policies and practices on employee attitudes and behavior. This study confirms that the psychological contract offers managers a useful framework within which to consider and manage the employment relationship

Coyle-Shapiro (2002) examined to understand how psychological contract affect employee behavior. For this purpose data were collected from 480 public sector employee. Hierarchical regression analysis was used to test the hypotheses and factor analysis was used to know the dimensions of OCB and for capturing the independent and moderator variables. Results revealed that the psychological contract is distinctive from other social exchange constructs that focus exclusively on the inducements received in the exchange relationship from the employees perspective. Loyalty behaviors are earned by the employer and not based on anticipatory employer behavior. Further this study suggests that employee engage in this type of citizenship behavior not to reciprocate the employer for present inducements but as a proactive step to facilitate the realization of future inducements

Conway and Briner (2002) determined the relationship between inconsistencies and inconclusiveness in work attitudes of full-time and part-time employees. This study tested the psychological contract as an explanatory framework for attitudinal differences across work status (i.e., whether employed on a part-time or fulltime basis). The model is tested across samples from two different organisations using structural equation modeling. The analysis reveals that part-time and full-time employees differed on a number of attitudes and that psychological contract fulfillment could be used to explain differences in certain attitudes (e.g., satisfaction) but not others (e.g., affective commitment). Analyses also show that the relationships between psychological contract fulfillment and outcomes were rarely moderated by work status, suggesting that part-time employees do respond in a similar way as full-time employees to adjustments in their psychological contract.

Coyle-Shapiro & Kessler (2002) explored reciprocity within the exchange relationship between the employee and employer through psychological contract framework. Further, this study examined the impact of the employer behavior in employee's obligation and fulfillment. For this purpose the longitudinal survey was conducted among 1400 employee and 84 managers working in public sector organisations. Hierarchical regression analysis was performed to analyze the data. The study reveals that perceived employer obligations at the first time is positively associated with employee's fulfillment of obligation, whereas at the second time perceived employer obligations at the first time is positively related to employee obligations and fulfillment of obligations at the second time.

Lambert, Edwards and Cable (2003) studied the relationship between employer–employee Breach and fulfillment in a psychological contract through traditional approach. In order to find the differences between the promised and delivered inducements and also to know its relations towards employee's satisfaction, they compared forecast derived from the conventional view as well as from an extended view. For this purpose longitudinal data was used and was analyzed through polynomial regression. Results proved that there is a little support for the traditional view and whereas, extended view revealed the relationships between breach and fulfillment results. Particularly, employee's satisfaction mainly depended neither in the increased inducement nor in the reduction of breach. Further employees satisfaction is positively related to the inducement what they received rather than what they promised

Dabos and Rousseau (2004) shared their beliefs regarding specific turns of the exchange and their reciprocal commitments. To perform this, data were collected from 96 scientist and 16 directors. Confirmatory factor analysis was performed in order to validate the psychological contract scale for staff scientists. The gap analysis revealed that the smaller gap indeed occurred on diagonal elements for all scales. Finally, result concluded that employer–employee mutuality and reciprocity in psychological contract were dyadic relationship and also this result supported the assumption of psychological contract theory

Kickul, Lester and Belgio (2004) responded to the call for more cross-cultural examinations of the psychological contract by investigating differences in: (a) the perceived importance of various psychological contract obligations, (b) the frequency of perceived psychological contract breach, and (c) employee attitudes and behaviors following psychological contract breach. A sample of sixty American and seventy-six Hong Kong Chinese employees completed measures related to the psychological contract, job satisfaction, and intention to turnover, organisational commitment, job performance, and organisational citizenship behaviors. Results showed that the employees from both cultures differed in terms of perceived psychological contract importance and breach. Specifically, the American workers placed higher importance and perceived less breach of both intrinsic and extrinsic psychological contract outcomes than the Hong Kong employees. Additionally, American employees responded more negatively to perceived breaches of intrinsic outcomes while their Hong Kong counterparts responded more negatively to perceived breaches of extrinsic outcomes.

Sutton and Griffin (2004) investigated the relationships among pre-entry expectations, post-entry experiences and psychological contract violations. The goal was to clarify the conceptual distinctions between the constructs and to test their differential impact on job satisfaction. In a national longitudinal study, 235 final-year occupational therapy students were surveyed immediately prior to entering the profession and again 14 months later. Post-entry experiences regarding supervision were found to predict psychological contract violation. Whereas the post-entry experiences the psychological contract violations were found to jointly predict the job satisfaction, with psychological contract violations demonstrating the stronger relationship. Pre-entry expectations positively correlated with job satisfaction, but this relationship was fully interceded by post-entry experiences. Met expectations, as measured by an interaction between pre-entry expectations and post-entry experiences, was not a predictor of psychological contract violation. Nor did met expectations predict job satisfaction after controlling for contract violations. The findings reinforce a positive relationship between job satisfaction and turnover. These findings supported the use of separate and proportionate measures of pre-entry expectations and post-entry experiences, and the integration of all three constructs in models of job satisfaction.

Coyle-Shapiro & Conway (2005) investigated the relationship between psychological contract, OCB and POS. For this purpose data was collected from 347 public sector employee. Factor analysis and regression analysis were performed to analyze the data. Finally, study reveals that components of psychological contract fulfillment and POS played a critical role in employee's organisational behavior.

Coyle-Shapiro, Morrow and Kessler (2005) examined the employment relationship of long-turn contracted employee through social exchange framework. Particularly, the research focused on the effects of employers POS from contracting and client organisation towards affective commitment to each organisation and service oriented citizenship behavior. Data were collected from 99 long-term contracted employee working for public service provider contracting organisation. Factor analysis and hierarchical regression analysis were performed to analyze the data. Hence, the study statistically proved that employee opinion of customer organisational supportiveness was significantly related to felt obligation and commitment to the customer organisation·

Coyle-Shapiro and Shore (2007) examined the status of Employee-Organisation relationship theory and its assumption and also investigated the under developed area in the EOR. Literature were presented with some attention towards the specifications of agents placing the EOR in context and also micro-macro levels of the EOR·

2.3   PSYCHOLOGICAL EMPOWERMENT

This section of the chapter discusses about the previous research on psychological empowerment and its impact on individual well-being.

Spreitzer (1996) examined the relationship between social structural characteristic of employee towards their feeling of empowerment and also measured the social characteristic perceptions of role ambiguity. Span of control socio political support access to information, resources and work unit climate at the level of work unit were adopted. For this purpose data were collected from 393 middle managers from different units of a fortune 50 organisation. Regression analysis and exploratory factor analysis were used to analyze the data. The study revealed that a work unit with little role ambiguity had a strong socio-political support access to information and participative unit climate was found to be significantly associated with managerial perception of empowerment and also, the boss who had a wide span of control·

Spreitzer, Kizilos and Nason (1997) examined the contribution of each of the four dimensions in Thomas and velthouse's (1990) multidimensional conceptualization of psychological empowerment effectiveness, work satisfaction and job related strain. The literature on the four dimensions of empowerment (meaning, competence, self determination and impact) was reviewed and theoretical logic was developed linking the dimensions to specific outcomes. The expected relationships were tested on a sample of managers from diverse units of a manufacturing organisation and then replicated on an independent sample of lower-level employees in a service organisation using alternative measures of the outcome variables. The results, largely consistent across the two samples, suggested that different dimensions were related to different outcomes and that no single dimension predicts all three outcomes. These results indicated that employees need to experience each of the empowerment dimensions in order to achieve all the hoped outcomes of empowerment·

Kirkman and Rosen (1999) examined the relationship between organisational and job characteristic, team empowerment and work team effectiveness. Further they investigated the antecedents, and consequences of team empowerment as well as the meditational role of empowerment. External team leader behavior, production and service responsibilities, team-based human resource policies and social structures were used to measure organisational and job characteristics. Potency, meaningfulness, autonomy and impact were considered as the dimensions of team empowerment. Performance outcome and attitudinal outcome were considered as the dimensions of work team effectiveness; further productivity, pro-activity and customer service was used to measure the performance outcome whereas job satisfaction, organisational commitment and team commitment was used to measure the attitudinal outcomes of the employee. For this purpose data were collected from 111 work teams in four organisations. The study revealed that highly empowered teams were more productive and proactive compared to less empowered teams which in-turn leads to higher level of customer service, job satisfaction and organisational as well as team commitment.

Spreitzer, Janasz and Quinn (1999) examined the relationship between psychological empowerment and leadership. Empowered supervisors were theorized to be innovative, upward influencing, and inspirational and less focused on monitoring to maintain the status quo. Tested sample of mid-level supervisors from a fortune 500 organisation, the hypotheses were largely supported. Supervisors who reported higher levels of empowerment were seen by their subordinates as more innovative, upward influencing, and inspirational. No relationship was found between supervisory empowerment and monitoring behaviors.

Houghton and Yoho (2005) developed and presented a contingency model of leadership and psychological empowerment that specified the circumstances and situations under which follower self-leadership should be encouraged. The model suggested that certain key contingency factors were included, such as follower development, situational urgency and task structure. Each specific leadership approach in-turn resulted in a specific combination of predictable outcomes, which included the level of follower involvement, dependence, creativity and psychological empowerment.

Ugboro (2006) designed to determine the relationship between job redesign, employee empowerment and intent to quit measured by affective organisational commitment among survivors of organisational restructuring and downsizing. It focused on middle level managers and employees in supervisory positions because survivors of this group are often called upon to assume expanded roles, functions and responsibilities in a post restructuring and downsizing environment. The results show statistically significant positive relationships between job redesign, empowerment and affective commitment. It therefore provides empirical data to support theoretical models for managing and mitigating survivors' intent to quit and subsequent voluntary turnover among survivors of organisational restructuring and downsizing.

Wang and Lee (2009) determined the interactive effects of the psychological empowerment dimensions on job satisfaction. Using data collected from employees of multiple organisations, the authors found intriguing three-way interactions among the dimensions.

Choice has a weak but negative effect on job satisfaction when both competence and impact are high or low but has a strong positive effect when one of the two dimensions is low and the other is high. Impact has no effect on job satisfaction when choice and competence are both high and both low. The effect of impact is positive only when one of the two dimensions is high and the other is low. In addition, high levels of choice and competence reinforce the positive effect of meaning on job satisfaction.

Lia, Toya, Lepak and Hong (2009) High-Performance Work Systems (HPWSs) have primarily examined the effects of HPWSs on establishment or firm-level performance from a management perspective in manufacturing settings. The study extended the literature by differentiating management and employee perspectives of HPWSs and examining how the two perspectives relate to employee individual performance in the service context. Data were collected in three phases from multiple sources involving 292 managers, 830 employees, and 1,772 customers of 91 bank branches. The data revealed significant differences between management and employee perspectives of HPWSs. There were also significant differences in employee perspectives of HPWSs among employees of different employment statuses and among employees of the same status. Further, employee perspective of HPWSs was positively related to individual general service performance. The mediation of employee human capital and perceived organisational support was positively related to individual knowledge-intensive service performance through the mediation of employee human capital and psychological empowerment. At the same time, management perspective of HPWSs was related to employee human capital and both types of service performance. Finally, all branch's overall knowledge-intensive service performance was positively associated with customers overall satisfaction with the branch's service.

Zhang and Bartol (2010) researched on Synthesizing theories of leadership, empowerment, and creativity tested a theoretical model linking empowering leadership with creativity via several intervening variables. The survey data from professional employees and their supervisors working at a large information technology company in China, found that empowering leadership positively affected psychological empowerment, which in-turn influenced both intrinsic motivation and creative process engagement. These latter two variables then had a positive influence on creativity. Empowerment role identity moderated the link between empowering leadership and psychological empowerment, whereas leader encouragement of creativity moderated the connection between psychological empowerment and creative process engagement.

Rawat (2011) explored the relationship between psychological empowerment and organisational commitment. For this purpose data were collected from 133 professional working in service sectors. Factor analysis and Regression analysis were used to analyze the data. The results show that psychological empowerment statistically influenced the three components of commitment, while measuring the impact of sub dimensions of empowerment on commitment dimension reveals that except in-case of normative commitment other 2 dimensions (Affective to continuance commitment) were influenced by sub dimensions of empowerment.

Thomas and Avijan Dutta (2011) examined the relationship between psychological empowerment and organisational commitment in the specific air-conditions industry. Further this study aimed at investigating the relevance of PE with organisational commitment. Data were collected from 71 managerial level employees. Analysis of variance was used to test the hypothesis. Paired sample correlation and regression analysis were also used to analyze the data. The results showed that the affective commitment contributes maximum to the psychological empowerment of the employee and therefore, such relationship could be derived.

Al-Swidi, Nawawi and Al Hosma (2012) examined the impact of transformational leadership between employee empowerment and job satisfaction. For this purpose data were collected from 160 employees working in Yemen Islamic Bank. Principal component analysis with varimax rotation and hierarchical regression analysis were used to analyze the data. The study statistically proved that there was a direct effect of employee psychological empowerment and the transformational leadership towards employee job satisfaction whereas the study did not support the moderating effects of transformational leadership towards the relationship between employee job satisfaction and their psychological empowerment.

Dimitriades and Kufidu (2004) examined the relationship between employment, empowerment and individual job organisation and industry factors in the Greek context. Data were collected from 163 mature working students attending business oriented PG programmes at the universities confirmatory factor analyses was used to investigate the multidimensional of the empowerment scale, correlation analysis was also used to understand the existence of a link between empowerment and its sub-scale. The study concludes that there is no statistical significant relationship between industry type and employment empowerment.

2.4   EMPLOYEE INVOLVEMENT

This section of the chapter deals with researches on Employee involvement in the management practice and its relationship towards employee's performance.

Mackie, Holahan and Gottlieb (2001) tested a theoretically driven model of the relationship between work environment, specifically, management practices, and employee mental health, specifically depression. It drew on theoretical perspectives connecting work environment and stress, and on others linking stress and depression. It also examines sense of coherence as a possible mediator of the relationships among work environment, work stress, and depression. Results showed that perceived exposure to employee involvement management practices was related to perceived work stress, sense of coherence, and depression. A model was specified to assess potential causal relationships using LISREL.

Chughtai (2008) examined the impact of job involvement on the self-report measures of in-role job performance and organisational citizenship behavior. The results of this study revealed that job involvement was positively correlated with both in-role job performance ($r = 0.30$, $p<0.01$) and OCB ($r = 0.43$, $p<0.01$). In addition to this it was found that organisational commitment partially mediated the job involvement performance relationship. Furthermore the findings of this research uncovered that job involvement exerted a stronger impact on OCB than on in-role performance. Finally the practical implications of this research for organisations were discussed.

Mohsan, Nawaz and Khan (2011) attempted to explore how Coaching has been gaining increasing attention from the organisational researchers as a recognized topic of scholarly study and is widely used by the financial institutions as a tool to enhance employees and ultimately organisational performance and productivity. The current study attempts to find the impact of coaching on the level of motivation and job involvement of employees working in banking sector of Pakistan. The data were collected from 285 banking personnel using the questionnaire as data collection instrument. A significant and positive correlation of coaching was found with employee motivation and job involvement. Some implications for future research are also drawn from the study.

Wood and De Menezes (2011) believed that the impact of high-performance work systems on employee's well-being are emerging but the underlying theory remained weak. The paper attempted to develop theory of the effects on well-being of four dimensions of high-performance work systems: enriched jobs, high involvement management, employee voice, and motivational supports. Theorized associations are tested using multilevel models and data from Britain's Workplace Employment Relations Survey of 2004 (WERS2004). Results show that enriched jobs are positively associated with both measures of well-being: job satisfaction and anxiety-contentment. Voice is positively associated with job satisfaction, and motivational supports with neither measure. The results for high involvement management are not as predicted because it increases anxiety and is independent of job satisfaction.

Ueda (2004) investigated the effects of job involvement, affective organisational commitment, and collectivism on organisational citizenship behavior (OCB) using data collected from 131 professors and clerical workers in a private Japanese university. Results show that job involvement had a significantly positive relationship on civic virtue and helping behavior, and affective organisational commitment had a significantly positive effect on helping behavior and sportsmanship. Collectivism also positively influenced civic virtue and helping behavior. In addition, the effect of affective organisational commitment on civic virtue was moderated by collectivism so that affective organisational commitment had a stronger effect when collectivism was weak than when collectivism was strong.

2.5 CULTURAL INTELLIGENCE

This section delineates previous researches that are related to cultural intelligent factors conceptualized at the individual level so as to promote a good work place behavior.

Kirkman and Shapico (2001) The mediating role of employee resistance test their earlier theoretical contention that employee resistance accounts for at least some of the relationship between cultural values and important work outcomes. Further this study investigated whether employee resistance to self-managing work team mediated the relationship between employee cultural values and job attitude and also to find the strength of mediation in each country for this purpose a field survey was conducted to collect 461 self managing work teams in four countries. Exploratory factor analysis and hierarchical regression analysis were performed to analyze the data. The result showed that resistance mediated the cultural value job attitude relationship. The study concluded that depending on the self management team cultural value job attitude relationship are sometimes fully or partly mediated by the resistance.

Triandis (2006) attempted to describe that successful interaction across culture required cultural intelligence. Several aspects of cultural intelligence in organisations were described suspending judgment until enough information about the other person becomes available, paying attention to the situation, cross-cultural training that increases isomorphic attributions, appropriate affect, appropriate behaviours, matching personal and organisationally attributes, increasing the probability of appropriate organisational practices.

Ang, Van Dyne and Koh (2006) examined relationships between Big Five personality and the four-factor model of cultural intelligence (CQ)— meta cognitive CQ, cognitive CQ, motivational CQ, and behavioral CQ. Hierarchical regression analyses conducted on data from 338 business undergraduates—after controlling the age, gender, and years of experience in interacting with people from other cultures—show significant links between (a) conscientiousness and meta cognitive CQ; (b) agreeableness and emotional stability with behavioral CQ; (c) extraversion with cognitive, motivational, and behavioral CQ; and (d) openness with all four factors of CQ.

The intriguing finding of this study is that openness was the only Big Five that was significantly related to all four aspects of CQ. This differs from prior research on openness that found few significant relationships. The results showed that openness to experience is a crucial personality characteristic that is related to a person's capability to function effectively in diverse cultural settings (CQ).

Templer, Tay and Chandrasekar (2006) explored the relationship of the motivational factor of cultural intelligence (CQ) and realistic previews to cross-cultural adjustment (work, general, and interaction adjustment) of global professionals. Regression analysis demonstrated the positive relationship between motivational CQ and all three adjustment criteria after controlling the gender, age, and time in the host country, and prior international assignment. Realistic job preview relates to work adjustment, realistic living conditions preview relates to general adjustment, and motivational CQ relates to work and general adjustment over and above realistic job and living conditions preview. The study demonstrated the importance and utility of motivational CQ by understanding the cross-cultural adjustment.

Ang, Van Dyne, Koh, Ng, Templer, Tay and Chandrasekar (2007) enhanced the theoretical precision of cultural intelligence (CQ: capability to function effectively in culturally diverse settings) by developing and testing a model that showed positive differential relationships between the four CQ dimensions (metacognitive, cognitive, motivational and behavioral) and three intercultural effectiveness outcomes (cultural judgment and decision making, cultural adaptation and task performance in culturally diverse settings). Before testing the model, they described development and cross-validation (N = 1,360) of the multidimensional cultural intelligence scale (CQS) across samples, time and country. They then described three substantive studies (N = 794) in field and educational development settings across two national contexts, the USA and Singapore. The results demonstrated a consistent pattern of relationships where Meta cognitive CQ and cognitive CQ predicted cultural judgment and decision making; motivational CQ and behavioral CQ predicted cultural adaptation and Meta cognitive CQ and behavioral CQ predicted task performance.

Van Dyne, Ang and Livermore (2009) theoretically demonstrated the importance of cultural intelligence and also the effectiveness of cross-cultural leadership further this study provided the four factor model of cultural intelligence and also four steps towards enhancing overall cultural intelligence.

Ng, Van Dyne and Ang (2009) investigated on experiential learning and cultural intelligence to propose a process model that focused on how leaders translate their international work assignment experiences into learning outcomes critical for global leadership development. This study model positions cultural intelligence as a moderator that enhances the likelihood that individuals on international assignments will actively engage in the four stages of experiential learning (experience, reflect, conceptualize, experiment), which in turn leads to global leadership self-efficacy, ethno relative attitudes toward other cultures, accurate mental models of leadership across cultures and flexibility of leadership styles. This model has major implications for the selection and training of individuals, as well as organisational practices related to international job assignments from a developmental perspective.

2.6 PSYCHOLOGICAL OWNERSHIP

This section of the chapter discusses about the previous studies on psychological ownership and its relationship towards Individual well-being and OCB

Van Dyne and Pierce (2004) examined the relationship between psychological ownership with employee work attitude and their citizenship behavior. Data were collected from 822 respondents which include 186 managers from the top 4 levels, 409 employees at top two levels and 227 professional employees from wide range of organisation. Confirmatory factor analysis and regression analysis were used to analyze the data. The results statistically proved that psychological ownership predicts two forms of OCB (supervisor and peer perceptions) over and above the two most commonly researched predictions of citizenship (satisfaction and commitment).

Mayhew, Ashkanasy, Bramble and Gardner (2007) examined psychological ownership in organisational settings related to the work attitudes of organisational commitment and satisfaction and also measured the impact of job autonomy as an antecedent to psychological ownership. Data were collected from 70 employees and by manager reported on the organisation and job based psychological ownership, organisational commitment. Job satisfaction, Perceived autonomy and organisation and job tenure managers/immediate supervisor's data were used to assess the in-role and extra-role behavior of each of their subordinates. Factor analysis and hierarchical multiple regression were used to analyse the data. The results statistically proved that there is no relationship between job and organisation based psychological ownership and helping or voice extra-role behavior.

Reb and Connolly (2007) examined the general assumption of judgment in decision making that ignored the distinction between actual and subjective feelings of ownership, tactically assuming that the two corresponded closely. This research suggested that the assumption might be usefully reexamined. In two experiments on the endowment effect they examined the role of subjective ownership by independently manipulating factual ownership (i.e., what participants were told about ownership) and physical possession of an object. This allowed them to disentangle the effects of the two factors, which are typically confounded. The study found a significant effect of possession, but not of factual ownership, on monetary valuation of the object. Moreover, this effect was mediated by participants' feelings of ownership, which were enhanced by the physical possession of the object.

Avey, Avolio, Crossley and Luthans (2009) viewed psychological ownership as a positive resource for impacting human performance in organisations; the present study investigated the components of an expanded view of psychological ownership. Confirmatory factor analyses on a proposed measure of psychological ownership provided support for a positively-oriented, "promotion-focused" aspect of psychological ownership comprised of four dimensions: self-efficacy, accountability, sense of belongingness and self-identity. In addition, territoriality was examined as a unique and more "prevention-focused" form of ownership. Practical implications and suggestions for future research on psychological ownership and positive organisational behavior concluded the article.

Chung and Moon (2011) examined the relationship between psychological ownership and constructive deviant behavior with an assumption that functional behavior intended to improve the organisation's well-being and also this research further examined the moderating effects of collectivistic orientation on psychological ownership and constructive deviant behavior. Data were collected from 465 employees working in industries and organisations varied on the basis of organisational characteristics. Confirmatory factory analysis and hierarchical multiple regression analysis were performed to analyze the data. Therefore, their research statistically proved that there was a relationship between psychological ownership and constructive deviant behavior.

2.7 PERCEIVED ORGANISATIONAL SUPPORT

There are bodies of research investigating POS and PSS as well research using student study. These studies are highly relevant to understand the effect of support perceived by the employees from their management.

Eisenberger, Huntington, Hutchison and Sowa (1986) answered the 3 main questions (i) employee from global beliefs concerning the extent to which organisation values their contributions and care about well being (ii) perceived organisational support reduces absenteeism and (iii) To know the relationship strength between perceived organisational support and employee absenteeism through employee exchange ideology through two studies i.e. (a) Globality of perceived organisational support and (b) Effects of POS and exchange ideology on absenteeism. Data were collected from 361 employees. Factor analysis, mean and standard deviation were compared to analyse the data. Therefore, result showed that there was a strong positive relationship between POS and commitment to the organisation.

Eisenberger, Fasolo, and Davis-LaMastro (1990) reported a positive relationship of employee's perception of being valued and cared about by the organisation with (a) conscientiousness in carrying out conventional job responsibilities, (b) expressed affective and calculative involvements in the organisation, and (e) innovation on behalf of the organisation in the absence of anticipated direct reward or personal recognition.

In the first Study, involving six occupations, positive relationships of perceived support with job attendance and performance were found. In the second Study, using manufacturing hourly employees and managers, perceived support was positively related to affective attachment, performance outcome expectancies, and the constructiveness of anonymous suggestions for helping the organisation. These results favored the extension and integration of emotion-based and calculative theories of organisational commitment into a social-exchange approach.

Shore and Wayne (1993) examined the social exchange view of commitment and suggested that employees perceptions of the organisation's commitment to them (perceived organisational support, or POS) creates feelings of obligation to the employer, which enhances the employees work behavior. The authors addressed the question of whether POS or the more conventional commitment concepts of affective commitment (AC) and continuance commitment (CC) were better predictors of employee behavior (organisational citizenship and impression management). Participants were 383 employees and their managers. Although results showed that both AC and POS were positively related to organisational citizenship and that CC was negatively related to organisational citizenship, POS was the best predictor. These findings support the social exchange view that POS creates feelings of obligation that contribute to citizenship behaviors. In addition, CC was unrelated, whereas AC and POS were positively correlated, with some impression on management behaviors.

Settoon, Bennett and Liden (1996) focused on the Social exchange (P. Blau, 1964) and the norm of reciprocity (A. W. Gouldner, 1960) in order to explain the relationship of perceived organisational support and leader-member exchange with employee attitudes and behavior. Recent empirical research suggests that individuals engage in different reciprocation efforts depending on the exchange partner. The study investigated these relationships by examining the relative contribution of indicators of employee-organisation exchange and subordinate-supervisor exchange. Structural equation modeling was used to compare nested models. Results indicate that perceived organisational support was associated with organisational commitment, whereas leader-member exchange was associated with citizenship and in-role behavior.

Eisenberger, Cummings, Armeli and Lynch (1997) surveyed diverse sample of 295 employees drawn from a variety of organisations to investigate (a) whether the relationship between the favorableness of job conditions and perceived organisational support (POS) depends on employee perceptions concerning the organisation's freedom of action and (b) whether POS and overall job satisfaction were distinct constructs. The favorableness of high-discretion job conditions was found to be much more closely associated with POS than was the favorableness of low-discretion job conditions. No such relationship was found between job conditions and satisfaction. To decide how much the organisation values their contributions and well-being, employees distinguish job conditions whose favorableness the organisation readily controls versus job conditions whose favorableness was constrained by limits on the organisation's discretion.

Armeli, Eisenberger, Fasolo and Lynch (1998) examined the relationship and strength between socio emotional needs and POS of police patrol officers. Further their study focused on the more discretionary activities of state police patrol officers making quests for driving under the influence of alcohol or drugs and issuing citations to speeders. For this purpose data were collected from 308 patrol officers. Factor analysis and regression analysis were performed to analyze the data. The study results explained that the employee satisfied with socio economic needs through caring, communication of respect and approval had the potential of markedly increasing their performance.

Lynch, Eisenberger and Armeli (1999) examined the relationship between inrole performance; Extra role performance and perceived organisational support, for this purpose data were collected from the retail sale employee. In order to investigate the moderating effect of POS on the relationship of employee fear of exploitation (reciprocation wariness) in exchange relationship and their impact on in-role and extra role performance of retail employee working in various organisations. Hierarchical regression analysis performed to assess the moderating effects of POS towards reciprocation wariness was negatively related to the in-role and extra role performance of retail employee.

Maignan, Ferrell and Hult (1999) explored the nature of corporate citizenship and its relevance for marketing practitioners and academic researchers. Specifically, conceptualization and operationalization of corporate citizenship were first proposed. Then, an empirical investigation conducted in two independent samples examined whether components of an organisation's culture affect the level of commitment to corporate citizenship and whether corporate citizenship is conducive to business benefits. Survey results suggested that market-oriented cultures as well as humanistic cultures lead to proactive corporate citizenship, which in turn are associated to improved levels of employee commitment, customer loyalty, and business performance. The results pointed the corporate citizenship as a potentially fruitful business practices both in terms of internal and external marketing.

Eisenberger, Armeli, Rexwinkel, Lynch and Rhoades (2001) investigated felt obligations contribution to the relationships of POS with affective organisational commitment, organisational spontaneity, in-role job performance and withdrawal behavior. Data were collected from 413 postal employees. Confirmatory factor analysis was used to model fit. Therefore, results showed that POS contributes to employee's felt obligation to care about the organisation's welfare and to act on behalf of the organisation in turn improved affective OC, organisational spontaneity and inrole performance.

Eisenberger, Stinglhamber, Vandenberghe, Sucharshki and Rhoades (2002) examined the relationship between employee temporal relationship between POS and PSS towards employee turnover. For this purpose 3 studies were investigated with 314 employee during the first study, 300 retail sales employees were surveyed during the second study and 493 retail sales employees were surveyed during the third study. Structural equation modeling was performed to analyze the data. During study – 1 PSS was significantly associated with temporal changes in POS. Study – 2 reveals that PSS – POS relationship increased with perceived supervisory status in the organisation. Study-3 reveals that POS mediated a negative relationship between PSS and employee turnover. These studies suggest that the position of the supervisor in the organisation contribute to POS which in-turn leads to job retention.

Aselage and Eisenberger (2003) mentioned that two theories - organisational support and psychological contract theories insists the importance of social exchange and maintenance of employer and employee relationship for an effective organisation; this study also focused on multiple dimension of this relationship. Further, this study identified the key dimensions of two theories and its power relationship explained by other theory and also explained the employer– employee relationship in an organisation. Researchers incorporated a report in which they highlighted the interdependence of perceived organisational support and the psychological contract.

Allen, Shore and Griffeth (2003) developed a model to investigate the antecedents of perceived organisational support (POS), and the role of POS in predicting voluntary turnover was developed and tested in two samples via structural equation modeling. Both samples of employees (N = 215 department store salespeople; N =197 insurance agents) completed attitude surveys that were related to turnover data collected approximately one year later. Results suggested that perceptions of supportive human resources practices (participation in decision making, fairness of rewards, and growth opportunities) contribute to the development of POS, and POS mediated their relationships with organisational commitment and job satisfaction. Further, POS is negatively related to withdrawal, but the relationships were also mediated.

Lew (2009) examined the relationship between POS felt obligation, affective commitment and turnover intention. Further study was supported by the social exchange theory, norms of reciprocity, POS theory. For this purpose data were collected from 134 full-time permanent teachers working in private higher educational institutions. Structural equations modeling were performed to analyze the data. The study proved that employee turnover intention was influenced by their affective commitment towards organisation.

2.8 IN-ROLE PERFORMANCE

The relationship between organisational support and inrole performance is a frequently studied question within the organisations. This section marks out the previous research examining the relationship between inrole performance and OCB.

Williams and Anderson (1991) investigated on the measurement and substantive issues. For this purpose data were collected from 127 supervisors and 334 employees of various organisations from a Mid

Western city. Factor analysis with oblique rotation was used to group the performance items. Hierarchical regression was also used to analyse the result. These results finally proved that three types of evidence that in role behavior, organisational citizenship behavior Individual and organisational citizenship behavior organisation were relatively distinct type of performance.

Werner (1994) examined the levels of in-role and extra role performance and experimentally manipulated a 3 X 2 in subject design. Dimensions capturing both in-role and extra role behaviors (i.e., citizenship behaviors directed toward other individuals) strongly influenced various measures of rater search strategies as well as the ratings given by 116 supervisors evaluating secretarial performance. A major finding of this study was the extent to which experienced raters sought and used information on both IRBs and OCBs. In regard to search by dimension, the dimensions of job knowledge, productivity, and attendance were viewed as most important for this job and organisation. Subjects sought this information earlier, and they sought more information on these dimensions than on the others. Despite the fact that dependability, attendance and following policies and procedures were both intended to capture citizenship behavior directed toward the organisation, the first OCBO dimension was treated more like the in-role dimensions, whereas the second OCBO dimension was treated more like the other extra role dimensions.

Diffendorff, Brown, Kamin and Lord (2002) based on their previous study examined a recent meta-analysis by Brown (1996) and concluded that job involvement was unrelated to job performance. The present investigation proposed that the null findings reported in this meta-analysis. The current study found that job involvement, when assed with a recent measure (pullay et al., 1994), was a significant predictor of supervisor ratings of Organisational Citizenship Behaviours and In-role Performance, controlling of work centrality and other individual difference variables. Consistent with findings, there was evidence that sex moderated some of the job involvement and OCB relationships, with females having a stronger, positive relationship between these constructs than male.

Turnley, Bolino, Lester and Bloodgood (2003) examined the relationships between psychological contract fulfillment and three types of employee behavior: in-role performance, organisational citizenship behavior directed at the organisation, and organisational citizenship behavior directed at individuals within the organisation. Using a sample of 134 supervisor-subordinate dyads, this study suggested that the extent of psychological contract fulfillment was positively related to the performance of all three types of employee behavior.

In addition, the results indicate that psychological contract fulfillment is more strongly related to citizenship behavior directed at the organisation than to citizenship behavior directed at one's colleagues. Finally, this research investigated if employee's attributions regarding the reasons that psychological contract breach occurred also impact their work performance. However, the data provided only limited support for the idea that employees are most likely to reduce their work effort when they perceive that the organisation has intentionally failed to live up to its commitments.

Vandaele and Gemmel (2006) examined the growing body of literature on different employee behaviors such as organisational citizenship behavior or boundary spanning behavior. Few research studies have investigated the impact of both in-role and extra-role behavior on performance outcomes, especially in business services settings. In this study they investigate how in-role behavior, extra-role behavior, and their interrelation influences employee performed productivity and quality in business security services. Data from 1,174 frontline service employees is analyzed using structural equation modeling. The results indicate that performance quality is directly influenced by in-role employee behavior oriented towards customers, while performance productivity is influenced by both in-role and extra-role employee behavior oriented towards employees and customers.

Colquitt, Scott, and LePine (2007) on the trust literature distinguished trustworthiness (the ability, benevolence, and integrity of a trustee) and trust propensity (a dispositional willingness to rely on others) from trust (the intention to accept vulnerability to a trustee based on positive expectations of his or her actions). Although this distinction had clarified some confusion in the literature, it remained unclear (a) which trust antecedents have the strongest relationships with trust and (b) whether trust fully mediated the effects of trustworthiness and trust propensity on behavioral outcomes. The meta-analysis of 132 independent samples summarized the relationships between the trust variables and both risk taking and job performance (task performance, citizenship behavior, counterproductive behavior). Meta-analytic structural equation modeling supported a partial mediation model wherein trustworthiness and trust propensity explained incremental variance in the behavioral outcomes when trust was controlled. Further analyses revealed that the trustworthiness dimensions also predicted affective commitment, which had unique relationships with the outcomes when controlling for trust. These results generalized across different types of trust measures (i.e., positive expectations measures, willingness-to-be-vulnerable measures, and direct measures) and different trust referents (i.e., leaders, coworkers).

Christensen and Whiting (2009) supported an empirical case that the importance of PSM was as much in its consequences as its existence. Specifically, they found that PSM was a significant moderator in the performance appraisal process. Raters with higher levels of PSM placed greater weight on helping behaviors in making their appraisal decisions. As hypothesized, their results suggest that high PSM raters provided a higher performance appraisal for high helpers, than did low PSM raters. Future research in this area might focus specifically on managers exhibiting the highest levels of PSM. Their results suggested the possibility that an alternative hypothesis may apply to these types of raters: OCBs will be expected so they will be rewarded less generously in the performance appraisal, and low OCBs will be strongly penalized. Second, with regards to OCB research this work began to inform what characteristics of the rater might moderate the relationship between OCBs and performance appraisals. To this point, the search for moderators of this relationship has been limited to characteristics of the ratee (gender, position in the organisational hierarchy) or the situation (low and high task interdependence).

The research began to inform how characteristics of the rater, and raters' individual differences might be important in determining how much weight raters will place on the performance of OCBs versus task behaviors in making their appraisal decisions.

Judge, Thoresen, Bono and Patton (2011) provided a qualitative and quantitative review of the relationship between job satisfaction and job performance was provided. The qualitative review is organized around 7 models that characterize past research on the relationship between job satisfaction and job performance. Although some models have received more support than others, research had not provided conclusive confirmation or disconfirmation of any model, partly because of a lack of assimilation and integration in the literature. Research devoted to testing these models decreased following 2 meta-analyses of the job satisfaction-job performance relationship.

Because of limitations in these prior analyses and the misinterpretation of their findings, a new meta-analysis was conducted on 312 samples with a combined N of 54.417. The mean true correlation between overall job satisfaction and job performance was estimated to be .30. In light of these results and the qualitative review, an agenda for future research on the satisfaction-performance relationship was provided.

Huang and You (2011) had thrown light on strong theoretical support for organisational commitment impact on in-role behaviors and organisational citizenship behavior performance. However, previous studies did not attain consistent conclusions with respect to the influence of organisational commitment on organisational citizenship behavior. The purpose of the study was to adopt the three components of organisational commitment scale of Meyer and Allen (1991) and followed the suggestions of Williams and Anderson (1991) to explore the influence of the three components of organisational commitment on in-role behaviors and two dimensions of organisational citizenship behavior (OCBI and OCBO). In conclusion, the research found that the three components of organisational commitment had a considerably important influence on in-role behaviors and two dimensions of organisational citizenship behavior (OCBI and OCBO).

2.9   PSYCHOLOGICAL WELL-BEING

This section in this chapter deals with the previous studies relates to the psychological well-being.

Warr, Cook and Wall (1979) examined the more number of individual perception had often direct researchers to originate new items or to select from existing measures subdivision with unknown psychological measurement. For this purpose two studies with 200 and 390 blue collar male workers were conducted. Factor analysis with varimax rotation and cluster analysis were used to analyze the data. The results proved that eight measures were acceptable for blue collar workers and their psychometric properties appear to be good.

Repetti (1987) explained the social origins of psychological well-being is limited by the possibility of reciprocal influences between persons and their social situations as well as by respondent bias. These issues are discussed in a study of the relation between the social environment at work and mental health. Two components of social environment were measured: a common social environment, the social climate shared by employees in the same work setting, and an individual social environment, the social space surrounding one individual in the setting. The study related (a) averaged co-workers' ratings and individuals' own ratings of the social environment to (b) individuals' self-reported psychological well-being. A group of 37 bank branches represented work environments, and non managerial personnel in the branches served as participants. Results indicated that the quality of the social environment at work is related to the mental health of the employees. More important, the relation was confirmed with an independent measure of the social environment. Aggregate co-worker ratings of the common social environment were significantly correlated with individual depression and anxiety. However, an individual's perceptions appeared to mediate the social environment's impact. As theorized, well-being was more closely tied to the proximal individual social environment than to the more distal common social environment.

Warr (1990) described new measures and aspects of mental health and presented baseline information for both male and female workers. Baseline data were presented from a sample of 1686 job holders and earlier uses of the well-being were summarized. Factor analysis and correlation analysis was adapted to analyze the data. The result proved that new scale appears to be psychometrically acceptable and was associated with demographic and occupational features.

Parker, Chmiel and Wall (1997) examined the effect of intentional rationalizing on work characteristics and also identified that employee well-being was mediated by the change in work characteristics during the rationalizing for this purpose. 4 years of longitudinal study was conducted. At first time the survey administered 455 employees on site. 4 years later second time survey administered 283 employees on site. Analysis of variance and hierarchical regression analysis were performed to analyze the data. The result showed that employee high demand for work characteristics was associated with poor quality of well-being but that increased in control, clarity and involvement were associated with better well-being.

De Jonge and Schaufeli (1998) examined the warr's comprehensive vitamin model empirically. For this purpose data were collected from 1437 Dutch health care workers. SEM was adopted to test the relationship between job characteristics and affective well being. Therefore, this study partially supported the assertion of the vitamin model that showed non-linear relationship between job characteristics and employee well being.

Jonge, Dormann, Janssen, Dollard, Landeweerd and Nijhuis (2001) described a two-wave panel study which was carried out to examine reciprocal relationships between job characteristics and work-related psychological well-being. Hypotheses were tested in a sample of 261 healthcare professionals using structural equation modeling (LISREL 8). Controlling for gender, age, and negative affectivity, the results primarily supported the hypothesis that Time 1 job characteristics influenced Time 2 psychological well-being. More specifically, Time 2 job satisfaction was determined by Time 1 job demands and workplace social support respectively. Furthermore, there was also some preliminary but weak evidence for reversed cross-lagged effects since Time 1 emotional exhaustion seemed to be the causal dominant factor with respect to Time 2 (perceived) job demands.

In conclusion, these studies build on earlier cross-sectional and longitudinal findings by eliminating confounding factors and diminishing methodological deficiencies. Empirical support for the influence of job characteristics on psychological well-being affirmed what several theoretical models have postulated to be the causal ordering among job characteristics and work-related psychological well-being.

Harter, Schmidt and Keyes (2002) concluded that the well being perspective is quite applicable to businesses and that, as managers and employees focus on satisfying basic human needs in the work place clarifying desired outcomes and increasing opportunity for individual fulfillment and growth they may increase the opportunity for the success of their organisation. The data indicated that workplaces with engaged employees, on average, do a better job of keeping employees, satisfying customers and being financially productive and profitable. Work place well being and performance were not independent. Rather, they were complimentary and dependent components of a financially and psychologically healthy workplace.

McKee-Ryan, Song, Wanberg and Kinicki (2005) used theoretical models to organize the diverse unemployment literature, and meta-analytic techniques. These were primarily used to examine the impact of unemployment on worker well-being across 104 empirical studies with 437 effect sizes. Unemployed individuals had lower psychological and physical well-being than their employed counterparts. Unemployment duration and sample type (school leaver vs. mature unemployed) moderated the relationship between mental health and unemployment, but the current unemployment rate and the amount of unemployment benefits did not. Within the unemployed samples, work-role centrality, coping resources (personal, social, financial, and time structure), cognitive appraisals, and coping strategies displayed stronger relationships with mental health than did human capital or demographic variables. The authors identified gaps in the literature and propose directions for future unemployment research.

Panaccio and Vandenberghe (2009) examined the relationships between perceived organisational support and organisational commitment with employee well-being. For this purpose longitudinal data were collected from 220 employees. Confirmatory factor analysis was used to test the hypotheses.

The result suggested that the exchange relationship between employee and his/her organisation and more specifically the resources derived from that relationship affect well-being beyond the impact of the workplace stressors.

Robertson and Cooper (2010) explained the relationship between employee full engagement and employee well-being. By adopting the Asset measurement model author gave a conceptual model to balance the leaders and managers support. Engagement as a single factors played a vital role in the employees well being and their commitment towards their work. Finally this research concluded that strong theoretical knowledge for practitioner and researchers will help them to measure the influencing dimensions of employee engagement.

Avey, Luthans, Smith and Palmer (2010) recognized core construct of psychological capital or PsyCap (consisting of the positive psychological resources of efficacy, hope, optimism, and resilience) had been demonstrated to be related to various employee attitudinal, behavioral, and performance outcomes. However, to date, the impact of this positive core construct over time and on important employee well-being outcomes had not been tested. The study fulfilled the need by analyzing the relationship between a broad cross-section of employees (N = 280) level of PsyCap and two measures of psychological well-being over time. The results indicated that employees PsyCap was related to both measures of well-being and, importantly, that PsyCap explained additional variance in these well-being measures over time.

Bockerman, Ilmakunnas and Johansson (2011) examined the effects of establishment- and industry-level labor market turnover on employees well-being. The linking between the employer-employee panel data contained both survey information on employee's subjective wellbeing and comprehensive register-based information on job and worker flows. The test for existence of compensating wage differentials was done by explaining wages and job satisfaction with average uncertainties, measured by an indicator for a high turnover (churning) rate. The results were consistent with the theory of compensating wage differentials, since high uncertainty increased real wages, but high uncertainty had no effect on job satisfaction while not controlling for wages.

2.10 ORGANISATIONAL COMMITMENT

This section in this chapter discusses the previous studies relates to Organisational commitment and its relationship towards organisational citizenship behavior.

Meyer, Allen and Smith (1993) tested the generalizability of organisational commitment 3-component model to the domain of occupational commitment. Measures of affective, continuance, and normative commitment to occupation were developed and used to test hypotheses concerning their differential relations with antecedent and consequence variables. Confirmatory factor analyses conducted on data collected from samples of student and registered nurses revealed that the 3 component measures of occupational commitment were distinguishable from one another and from measures of the 3 components of organisational commitment. Results of correlation and regression analyses were generally consistent with predictions made on the basis of the 3-component model and demonstrated that occupational and organisational commitment contribute independently to the prediction of professional activity and work behavior.

Moynibah, Boswell and Boudreau (2000) examined the impact of job satisfaction and dimensions of organisational commitment towards employee intention to leave search activity Performance and leadership effectiveness of executives. Data were collected from 803 executives and path analysis was performed to analyze the data. Therefore, results revealed that job satisfaction was positively related to performance but it is not with leadership. Continuance commitment negatively relates to performance as well as for leadership.

Meyer, Stanley, Herscovitch, and Topolnytsky (2002) conducted Meta analysis to assess the relations among affective, continuance and normative commitment to the organisation and relationship between three forms of commitment and variables identified as their antecedents, correlates and consequence of three component model. The results of Meta analysis provided the true relationship between the component and subcomponents of commitment and also variables identified as antecedents, consequences and correlates in this 3 component model.

Baruch and Winkelmann-Gleed (2002) examined different work-related focus of commitment, such as the work group and the employing organisation as well as the current occupation. It assesses how these focuses of commitment were influenced by, and influence, attitudes and emotions at work. Data from employees and managers in the British health-service sector shed light on the associations. Regression analysis revealed a strong association between positive works related emotions and commitment levels, leading to a higher intention to stay with the organisation.

Babaleus, Yavas, Karatepe and Avci (2003) tested the service recovery performance model further to analyze the relationship between management commitment to service quality which was nothing but the employee appraisal. Affective outcomes i.e., employee emotional response and performance outcomes i.e., their behavior, training, empowerment and reward were used as the dimensions of appraisal. For this purpose data were collected from 180 frontline bank employees in Turkey. Confirmatory factor analysis was used to analyze the data. The result suggested that top management commitment to service quality as manifested by frontline employee appraisal of training empowerment and rewards had a positive effect on their perceptions of service recovery performance. Therefore, the influence of MCSQ on service recovery performance was mediated by employee job satisfaction and their affective commitment towards the organisation.

Ito and Brotheridge (2005) investigated the link between employee's participation in decision making (PDM), autonomy and supervisory career support towards career adaptability and affective commitment which in-turn lead to employees dependence towards the organisation or lead to employees turnover intention. In order to test this model data were collected from 680 Canadian federal civil service employee. Exploratory and confirmatory factor analysis was performed to analyze the data. The result statistically proved that PDM, autonomy and supervisory support positively lead to commitment and negatively towards intention to leave, whereas career adaptability positively leads to intentions to quit.

Çelik (2008) examined the relationship between components of organisational commitment and job satisfaction of tax Office employees. Factor analysis was conducted on the data obtained through organisational commitment scale developed by Meyer and Allen (1990). Cronbach's alpha coefficient and also test item total correlation were calculated for reliability of the factors. For two groups comparisons Mann Whitney u test and more than two group's comparisons Kruskall Wallis test were used to analyze the data. It was assumed that there had not been any similar research conducted on tax Office employees and that therefore this study could make important contribution to an extant research in management and organisational behavior.

Uygur and Kilic (2009) studied the level of organisational commitment and the job involvement of the personnel at Central Organisation of Ministry of Health in Turkey. 210 subjects, selected randomly, were distributed the questionnaire forms. Of the questionnaires, 180 of them (86%) returned and 168 of them were regarded as valid and acceptable and analyzed. A moderate positive correlation was found out between organisational commitment and job involvement (r=0.44). In the light of this, there was a significant correlation between organisational commitment and job involvement, though not very strong.

Kim, Tavitiyaman and Kim (2009) focused on the effect of four management commitments to service factors (i.e., organisational support, rewards, empowerment, and training) on employee's job satisfaction and service behaviors. Ten hotels, located in Bangkok, the capital of Thailand, participated in this study. The structural equation model was used. Thai hotel workers indicated that rewards, empowerment, and training were positively related to job satisfaction but did not support a path from organisational support for job satisfaction. The positive impact of empowerment on employee's job satisfaction in a high power distance culture such as Thailand was an unexpected finding. It may result from proper training and reward systems offered to young Thai frontline employees who were familiar with and favor U.S. (Western) culture. In summary, this study showed that job satisfaction serves as a mediator between three management service initiatives (rewards, empowerment, and training) and employees' service behaviors toward customers and co-workers.

Kuean, Kaur and Wong (2010) examined the relationship between organisational commitment and employee's intention to leave the organisation in a Malaysian situation and included the moderating effects of decision making participation and the employee's work-effort on the employee-employer relationship, as well as on their work effort. This study had two objectives, firstly to establish the relationship between organisational commitment and intentions to leave among working adults in Malaysia. Secondly, was to investigate the moderating effect of decision making participation and the effort needed to express an intention to leave by these same adults. This was a descriptive study based on a 300 sample size survey conducted among working adults in Malaysia. There were 189 responses received representing a response rate of 63%. Of these only 181 responses with no missing values were used for data analysis as the others were rejected as being incomplete. The correlation analysis resulted from this study confirmed previous researcher's observations linking higher organisation as the most important predictor of intention to leave. Employees were less likely to leave when they had an emotional commitment and to identify with their organisation. Cultivating an organisational culture of shared values and involving employees in the goal setting processes would further enhance employee's acceptance of and alignment with stated Organisational goals. This promoted a greater personal organisational commitment and eventually reduces employee's intentions to leave the organisation.

Liu and Cohen (2010) examined the relationship between individual values, Organisational and occupational commitment and OCB and inrole performance between Chinese employee and western employee data were collected from 166 employees working in public sector organisations in Northern China. Hierarchical regression analysis was used to analyze the data. The result showed the strong negative relationship between self directions and dimensions commitment. Further in-case of OCB the result showed the negative effect of achievement on achievements. Therefore, the study suggested that Chinese culture looks at the concepts different by than do western observers. Western samples were arrived from previous studies.

Shah and Shah (2010) tried to explore the relationship between predictive power of supervisor and peers. Further this study examined the employees attitude, beliefs and behaviors to readiness for organisational change. For investigation purpose 556 full-time faculty members working at various level in public sector organisation were selected. Pearson correlation analysis, Regression Analysis and Multivariate analysis of variances were performed to analyze the data. The study finalized that attitude of young employees were positively related to readiness to change their job.

Abdullah (2011) examined the Organisational Commitment comprises of three distinguishable components: Affective, Continuance and Normative Commitment. The study aimed at evaluating Construct Validity (Convergent and Discriminant Validity) and Internal Reliability for Allen and Meyer's Organisational Commitment Scale (1996) among the Banking Sector employees of Pakistan. The study was the first of its kind in a Pakistani setting. Eighteen items (6 for each of the three measures of Affective, Continuance and Normative Commitment) were used in the questionnaire. Two hundred and fifteen (215) valid responses from Major cities of Pakistan were analyzed for this study. The study revealed that the three measures (Affective, Continuance and Normative) were distinguishable from each other, on the basis of Construct Validity and Internal Reliability Analysis. This validated that Allen and Meyer's Organisational Commitment measures can be applied in Pakistani culture also.

2.11   ORGANISATIONAL CITIZENSHIP BEHAVIOR

This section in this chapter discusses the previous studies relating to OCB and its relationship towards dimensions of ERM.

Moorman, Niehoff and Organ (1993) analyzed the effects of job satisfaction, organisational commitment and procedural justice and also assessed the relationship between job fairness, job satisfaction, organisational commitment and organisational citizenship. Data were collected from 420 employee of a national cable company. Structured equation modeling was used to isolate and describe the path between the 3 job attitudes and OCB and among procedural justice, job satisfaction and commitment.

Finally, result showed that there were significant associations between fairness, commitment, and justice towards 3 dimensions of OCB whereas affective commitment, continuance commitment and work satisfaction to the dimensions of OCB were insignificant. Further, this study suggested that by improving the fair treatment and fair procedures towards employee results in key antecedent to promoting OCB performance conscientiousness employee towards their work and in-turn they try to prevent problems with other employee.

Allison, Voss and Huston (2001) researched the impact of social-desirability response bias (SDB) on the relationship between organisational citizenship behavior (OCB) and two measures of student performance (productivity, cumulative GPA) were explored. Hierarchical regression analysis demonstrated the various dimensions of OCB. This study suggested that some components of OCB do indeed lead to greater individual performance. Furthermore, these findings strongly indicate that research into OCB must incorporate a measure of SDB in order to control the inflation in self-reported OCB scores that was likely to occur. In this study, failure to control SDB would have concealed some critical evidence demonstrating relationships between OCB and performance that could be of great value in both research and in practical applications.

Cardon and Espejo (2002) compared the ratings of 3 dimensions of OCB rated by manager (self) to their subordinates and to their colleagues (superiors and peers) in the Spanish branch of a multinational food company. For this purpose data were collected from 73 managers, 73 supervisors, 179 peers and 209 subordinates. Hierarchical confirmatory factor analysis was performed to identify the dimensions of OCB. In most of the cases subordinate and self-ratings were significantly higher than colleague rating.

Farh, Zhong and Organ (2004) explored the importance of OCB employee behavior and actions that were not specifically designated in their formal job duties. For the research purpose data were collected from 158 employees and 72 managers working in industries and technological enterprises. Inductive approach was used to identify the major dimensions of OCB in China. Content analysis and logistic regression was also used to analyze the data. Therefore, results proved that organisation influence the dimensions of OCB.

Emmerik, Jawahar and Stone (2005) examined the relationships among altruism, burnout and a positive outcome, namely, the engagement in organisational citizenship behavior. Web questionnaires were distributed to employees in three professional organisations. The results from the 178 respondents indicated that altruism is related to organisational citizenship behavior. Of the three dimensions of burnout, only reduced personal accomplishment was (negatively) associated with engagement in organisational citizenship behaviors.

Podsakoff, Whiting, Podsakoff and Blume (2009) provided a meta-analytic examination of the relationships between OCBs and a variety of individual and organisational-level outcomes. Results, based on 168 independent samples (N = 51,235 individuals), indicated that OCBs were related to a number of individual-level outcomes, including managerial ratings of employee performance, reward allocation decisions, and a variety of withdrawal-related criteria (e.g., employee turnover intentions, actual turnover, and absenteeism). In addition, OCBs were found to be related (k =38; N = 3,611 units) to a number of organisational level outcomes (e.g., productivity, efficiency, reduced costs, customer satisfaction, and unit level turnover). Of interest, somewhat stronger relationships were observed between OCBs and unit level performance measures in longitudinal studies than in cross-sectional studies, providing some evidence that OCBs were causally related to these criteria. The Meta analysis indicates that OCBs had significant relationships with a variety of individual and organisational-level outcomes.

Farzianpour, Foroushani, Kamjoo and Hosseini (2011) evaluated the mean organisational behavior score among the managers of the hospitals affiliated to Shahid Sadoughi University of Medical Sciences and Health Services, Yazd. A descriptive-analytic cross-sectional study was conducted on 117 managers in various organisational levels working at the study hospitals who were randomly selected. Questionnaire was used. The validity and reliability are approved by the university management professors and Cronbach's alpha coefficient of 0.70, respectively. All the questions were presented in a Likert scale with five options measuring four dimensions: (A) Generosity (B) Civil behavior (C) Conscious (D) Friendship. The data was entered in the SPSS software and Fisher exact test/chi-square test were used for data analysis. The mean age of the study population was 39 years among whom 66.7% were male and 33.3% were female. The working experience of the study population was at an average of 15.6 years. A total of 78 (66.7%) managers were educated in medicine, allied medicine and basic sciences. Considering the scores in different components of organisational behavior, generosity was placed first with a mean score of 12.3 and consciousness was placed fourth with a mean score of 5.47. Therefore there was a statistically significant association between sex, education level and the field of study being placed in certain quartiles of OCBs domains (p<0.05).

Ehtiyar, Alan and Oemueris (2010) showed that an individual's pro-social behavior affects an organisation's productivity. But unfortunately institutions that gave tourism education do not have enough importance to OCB. In this research, theoretical structure of OCB is analyzed and it was found out that there was an important relation between Akdeniz University, School of Tourism and Hotel Management's students' academic success and demographic aspects. It was found that there was a significant relation between the levels of students' organisational citizenship behavior and liking of their school. One other important result of the research was that there was a positive correlation between average grades of students and organisational citizenship behavior (R=0.190). It was found that those students who liked organisations, committed to them and do volunteer jobs were successful in their classes.

Mohsan et al., (2011) examined the impact of job involvement on organisational citizenship behavior (OCB) and in-role job performance of employees working in he banking sector of Pakistan. The data was collected from 112 subjects using the questionnaire forms and then Microsoft Excel and SPSS 16 was used for data analysis. The findings of the study revealed that job involvement was positively correlated with both organisational citizenship behavior (OCB) and in-role job performance but the relative impact of job involvement on OCB is stronger than on in-role job performance.

2.12   AN OVERVIEW

Summarizing the results of these studies it can be stated that ERM dimensions have indeed a positive effect on individual well-being and their work place behavior. The review about research on employee relationship management and their relationship towards the individual well-being and individual work place behavior, existing studies that controlled for ERM dimensions such as psychological contract, empowerment, employee involvement, cultural intelligence, organisational support, psychological ownership and inrole performance also found significant relationship between ERM variables and Individual well-being and OCB.

   Based on the review of literature it is established that the psychological contract, Cultural intelligence, psychological ownership has a positive effect on individual work place behavior. Psychological empowerment showed positive effects on Individual well-being i.e., psychological well-being and organisational commitment. Employee involvement, perceived organisational support and inrole performance positively impact both individual well-being and their work place behavior. The review on relationship between job attitudes, individual well-being and their work place behavior and it is mostly mediated by the inrole performance.

Though there is sufficient research evidence of relationship between variables and many studies have shown the importance of individual well-being and work outcomes. Only few systematic studies have provided empirical evidence of relationship between employer-employee relationship towards individual well-being and individual work place behavior. Most of the studies have concentrated on psychological contract or psychological empowerment or employee involvement or cultural intelligence or psychological ownership or perceived organisational support or inrole performance separately towards individual well-being or individual work place behavior and not extended in measuring the effects of all the above-mentioned variables towards individual well-being and their work place behavior.

In the light of the above discussion this book aims to fill the research gap by measuring comprehensive set of ERM dimensions towards individual well-being and individual work place behavior from both employees and managers perception.

3

ERM THEORIES

3.1 INTRODUCTION

Employee Relationship Management (ERM) is considered as an important motivational tool in order to make employees' active participation in the management. "The Formal Theory of Organisation" by Barnard clearly explained the key elements for an effective organisation. The following were the key elements:

- Communication: In order to achieve the common purpose with the existence of persons willing to contribute their skills and capabilities towards such purpose are the opposite pole of the system of cooperative effort. The process by which these potentialities become dynamic is through communication. The method of communication might be oral, written or in common language.

- Willingness to serve: The willingness required the belief that the purpose can be carried out, a faith that diminishes to the vanishing point as it appear that it is not in fact in process of being attained. Hence, when effectiveness ceased, willingness to contribute disappeared. The continuance of willingness also depends upon the satisfaction that was secured by individual contributors in the process of carrying out the purpose. If the satisfaction does not exceed scarifies then willingness disappears, whereas if satisfaction exceeds scarifies then willingness persist.

- Common purpose: The objective of the organisation is an act of cooperation. Common purpose is necessarily an internal, personal, subjective thing even though individual interpretation of it is subjective. The one exception to this general rule, an important one, is that the accomplishment of an organisation purpose becomes itself a source of personal satisfaction and a motive for many individuals in many organisations.

Further "The Theory of Organisational Equilibrium" by Bernard and Simon was considered as an essential theory of motivation in which they explained the importance of organisational inducement towards its member to continue their participation and hence assure organisational survival. The following are the features of the Equilibrium Theory.

1. An organisation is the system of interrelated social behaviors of a number of persons whom they call it as participants in the organisation.

2. Each participant and each group of participants receive inducements from the organisation and in-turn for which he makes contributions to the organisation.

3. Each participants will continue his participation in an organisation only so long as the inducements offered to him are as great or greater (measured in terms of his value and in terms of the alternatives open to him) than the contributions he is asked to make.

4. The contributions provided by the various groups of participants are the source from which the organisation manufactures the inducements offered to participants.

5. Hence, an organisation is solvent – and will continue in existence only so long as the contributions are sufficient to provide inducements in large enough measure to draw forth these contributions.

Therefore Theory of Formal Organisation and Theory of Organisational equilibrium were considered to be most important theories in employee relationship management. These theories helped to identify a conceptual model to analyze the relationship between employee and managers working in the public sector bank towards their well-being, level of commitments and their behavior at work place. Based on the above discussion following theories were identified and also briefly discussed in this chapter.

3.2 PSYCHOLOGICAL CONTRACT

Conceptual Definition

The Theory of Equilibrium Barnard's (1938) is one of the basic foundations of the psychological contract which assumed that employees continued participation depends on adequate rewards from the organisation. Therefore the theory sparked the idea of a give-and-take exchange underlying the employee-organisation relationship. Similarly Social Exchange theory Blau (1964) distinguished social from economic exchange along with various aspects: specificity of contract, moment frame work and also the reciprocity. In short, economic exchange is nothing but the expectation of both employer and employee at their work place in order to fulfill the expectation within that stipulated time. The concept of psychological contract had been derived from the "Understanding of organisational behavior" Argyris (1960). This theory explained psychological contract as an implicit understanding between the group of employees and their foreman. This theory assumed that employees would perform at higher level, if the organisation did not interfere too much with the employee groups norm and in return employees would respect the right of the organisation to evolve and also this theory defines psychological contract as an exchange of definite and beginning economic resources agreed by the two parties to fulfill each other's needs.

Operational Definition

A psychological contract is an individual's belief in mutual obligations between that person and another party, such as an employer (Rousseau, 1989). Psychological contracts can be operationalized from a variety of perspectives. A first cut on operationalization occurs with the decision whether or not to focus on aspects of the psychological contract believed to generalize across persons and settings. A second cut on the operationalization of psychological contracts occurs with the decision of whether to focus upon content, features and evaluations (Rousseau & Tijoriwala, 1998).

The content of psychological contracts refers to the terms and elements which comprise the contract (e.g., specific obligations such as job security, or general types of obligations such as relational or transactional). Features of psychological contracts characterize them on some element or attribute (e.g., explicit or implicit, stable or unstable over time).Evaluations assess the degree of fulfillment change or violation experienced within the context of the psychological contract.

Relational long-term or open-ended employment arrangements based upon mutual trust and loyalty. Rewards are only loosely conditioned on performance, derived from membership and participation in the organisation.

- **Stability**   Employee is obligated to remain with the firm and to do what is required to keep the job. Employer has committed to offering stable wages and long-term employment.

- **Loyalty**   Employee is obligated to support the firm, manifest loyalty and commitment to the organisation's needs and interests. Employee is obligated to be a good organisational citizen. Employer has committed to supporting the well-being and interests of employees and their families.

Balanced dynamic and open-ended employment arrangements conditioned on economic success of firm and worker opportunities to develop career advantages. Both worker and firm contribute highly to each other's learning and development. Rewards to workers are based upon performance and contributions to firm's comparative advantages, particularly in face of changing demands due to market pressures.

- **External** Employability   In the career development on the external labor market, employee is obligated to develop marketable skills and knowledge. Employer has committed to enhancing worker's long-term employability outside the organisation as well as within it.

- **Internal Advancement**   Career development within an internal labor market, employee is obligated to develop skills valued by this current employer. Employer has committed to creating worker career development opportunities within the firm.

- **Dynamic Performance** Employee is obligated to successfully perform new and more demanding goals, which can change again and again in the future, to help the firm become and remain competitive. Employer has committed to promote continuous learning and to help employees successfully execute escalating performance requirements.

Transactional employment arrangements with a short-term or limited duration, primarily focused upon economic exchange; specific, narrow duties and limited worker involvement in organisation.

- **Narrow** Employee is obligated to perform only a fixed or limited set of duties, to do only what he or she is paid to do. Employer has committed to offer the worker only limited involvement in the organisation, little or no training or other employee development.

Transitional It is not a psychological contract form itself, but a cognitive stated reflecting the consequences of organisational change and transitions that is at odds with a previously established employment arrangement.

- **Mistrust** When an Employee feels that the firm sends inconsistent and mixed signals regarding its intentions, employee mistrusts the firm. It is the manager withheld important information passed on by the employees. Firm mistrusts its workers.

- **Uncertainty** Employee is uncertain regarding the nature of his or her own obligations to the firm. Employer measure assesses the extent that the employee is uncertain regarding the employer's future commitments to him or her.

- **Erosion** Employee expects to receive fewer future returns from his or her contributions to the firm compared to the past; but contrary to this if the employer instituted changes that reduce employee wages, benefits this in-turn erodes the quality of work life compared to previous years.

- **Employee fulfillment** refers to the work obligated by the managers fulfilled by their employees.

- **Employer fulfillment** refers to the work obligated by the employees fulfilled by their managers.

3.3 PSYCHOLOGICAL EMPOWERMENT

Conceptual Definition

The Empowerment process Theory (Conger & Kanungo 1988) was derived from the two main theories, first Power-Dependence theory (R.M. Emerson 1962) which considered both persons and groups as actors in a power-network. Power is primarily a relational concept used to describe the perceived power or control that an individual actor or organisational subunit had over others. Social relations commonly entail ties of mutual dependence between the parties. The theory dictated exactly four generic types of balancing process, and discussion of these lead directly into processes of group formation, including the emergence of group norms, role structure and status hierarchy, all presented as the outcome of balancing tendencies in power relations. Outcome of this theory insisted two main directions by considering potential influence as the power and motivational Investment as the dependency. Secondly, Self efficacy Theory (1986) the strength of peoples' by Bandura suggested that conviction in their own effectiveness was likely to affect whether they would even try to cope with the given situations. They get involved in activities and behave assuredly when they judge themselves capable of handling situations that would otherwise be intimidating. Efficacy expectations determined how much effort people will expend and how long they will persist in the face of obstacles and aversive experiences. Therefore the empowerment process theory defined the empowerment as a process of enhancing feelings of self-efficacy among organisational members through the identification of conditions that faster powerlessness and through their removal by both formal organisational practice and informal techniques of providing efficacy information.

Operational Definition

Conger & Kanungo define empowerment as a motivational factor which as meaning to enable rather than simply delegates. Further empowerment is defined more broadly as increased intrinsic task motivation manifested in a set of four cognitions reflecting an individual's orientation to his or her work role: meaning, competence, self determination and impact.

Meaning   Meaning is the value of a work goal or purpose, judged in relation to an individual's own ideals or standards (Thomas & Velthouse, 1990) Meaning involves a fit between the requirements of a work role and beliefs, values and behaviors (Brief & Nord, 1990 ; Hackman & Oldham, 1980).

Competence   Competence or self-efficacy is an individual's belief in his/her capability to perform activities with skill (Gist, 1987). Competence is analogous to agency beliefs, Personal mastery, or effort performance expectancy (Bandura, 1989).

Self-determination   Where competence is a mastery of behavior, self-determination is an individual's sense of having choice in initiating and regulating actions (Deci, Connell & Ryan, 1969). Self-determination reflects autonomy in the initiation and continuation of work behaviors and processes; examples are making decisions about work methods, pace and effort (Bell & staw, 1989; spector, 1986)

Impact   Impact is the degree to which an individual can influence strategic, administrative of operating outcomes at work (Ashfo rth, 1989). Impact is the converse of learned helplessness (Martinko & Gardner, 1982). Further, Impact is different from locus of control. Whereas impact is influenced by the work context, internal locus of control is a global personality characteristic that endures across situations (Wolfe & Robertshaw, 1982).

3.4   EMPLOYEE INVOLVEMENT

Conceptual Definition

High involvement management was a term first introduced by Ed Lawler as an organisational approach mainly focused on employee involvement. Further it gave the employee an opportunity to act independently, to make decisions regarding the behavior of his/her jobs and further to take part in the business as a whole. Job-level involvement means increasing the decision making opportunities people had in their work, while organisational-level involvement, or empowerment, means giving employees a role in decisions concerned with strategy, investment and other major organisational matters.

Operational Definition

According to Lawler (1988), the three approaches to involvement are (1) parallel suggestion involvement, (2) job involvement, and (3) high involvement. They differ in the degree to which they direct that four key features should be moved to the lowest level of an organisation. The parallel suggestion approach does the least to move power, information, rewards and knowledge downward, while the high involvement approach does the most. Because they position power, information, knowledge and reward differently, these approaches tend to fit different situations and to produce different results.

Information   It is about the performance of the organisation, in other words Information is considered as affairs that are related to the rights and obligations of employees or the transfer of knowledge and other affairs that can be communicated between the management and employees.

Rewards   Egalitarian skill-based pay; gain sharing and/or profit sharing; employee ownership that are based on the performance of the organisation. In other words reward is consider as an important element that affects the outcome of employee involvement, which is the feedback for employees to acquire power, information, and knowledge.

Knowledge   It enables employees to understand technique, capability and professional knowledge of employees and contribute to organisational performance.

Power   It is to make decisions that influence organisational direction. In other words Distribution of the decision making power (i.e. the extent of democratization) in an organisation.

3.5   CULTURAL INTELLIGENCE

Conceptual Definition

The concept of Cultural intelligence is obtained by adopting the two theories. First, Kolb's (1984) experiential learning theory (ELT) is an adult learning theory that highlights the critical role experience plays in affecting learning and change. Formulation of ELT drew on the work of prominent educational and organisational scholars including John Dewey, Kurt Lewin, and Jean Piaget, who share the common view that learning involves integrating experience with concepts and linking observations to actions. To explicate the processes that enable leaders to learn and develop their global leadership capabilities through their international work assignments. Second, Sternberg and Detterman's (1986) framework of multiple intelligences, which integrates different perspectives of intelligence to propose four complementary ways of conceptualizing individual-level intelligence offer a more comprehensive theory of intelligence that goes beyond cognitive abilities such as linguistic or logical mathematical intelligence.

Operational Definition

Cultural intelligence (CQ), defined as an individual's capability to function and manage effectively in culturally diverse settings, is consistent with Schmidt and Hunter's (2000) definition of general intelligence as 'the ability to grasp and reason correctly with abstractions (concepts) and solve problems.' Although early research tended to view intelligence narrowly as the ability to solve problems in academic settings, there is now increasing consensus that intelligence may be displayed in places other than the classroom (Sternberg and Detterman, 1986). This growing interest in 'real world' intelligence includes intelligence that focused on specific content domains such as social intelligence (Thorndike and Stein, 1937), emotional intelligence (Mayer et al., 2000) and practical intelligence (Sternberg et al., 2000). CQ acknowledges the practical realities of globalization (Earley and Ang, 2003) and focuses on a specific domain – intercultural settings. Thus, following Schmidt and Hunter's (2000) definition of general intelligence, CQ is a specific form of intelligence focused on capabilities to grasp reason and behave effectively in situations characterized by cultural diversity.

Metacognitive CQ is an individual's cultural consciousness and awareness during interactions with those from different cultural backgrounds. The metacognitive factor of CQ is a critical component for at least three reasons. First, it promotes active thinking about people and situations when cultural backgrounds differ. Second, it triggers critical thinking about habits, assumptions and culturally bound thinking. Third, it allows individuals to evaluate and revise their mental maps, consequently increasing the accuracy of their understanding.

Cognitive CQ is an individual's cultural knowledge of norms, practices and conventions in different cultural settings. Given the wide variety of cultures in the contemporary world, cognitive CQ indicates knowledge of cultural universals as well as knowledge of cultural differences. The cognitive factor of CQ is a critical component because knowledge about cultural similarities and differences is the foundation of decision making and performance in cross-cultural situation.

Motivational CQ is an individual's capability to direct attention and energy toward cultural differences. Using the expectancy-value framework of motivation, we conceptualize motivational CQ as a special form of self-efficacy and intrinsic motivation play an important role in CQ because successful intercultural interaction requires a basic sense of confidence and interest in novel settings.

Behavior CQ is an individual's capability to exhibit appropriate verbal and nonverbal actions when interacting with people from different cultural backgrounds. Behavioral CQ is based on having and using a broad repertoire or range of behaviors. Behavioral CQ is a critical component of CQ because behavior is often the most visible characteristic of social interactions. In addition, nonverbal behaviors are especially critical because they function as a "silent language" that conveys meaning in subtle and covert ways (Hall, 1959).

3.6 PSYCHOLOGICAL OWNERSHIP

Conceptual Definition

There is diverse literature that suggests that the psychology of possession is well rooted in people socialized by a Western heritage. The psychological aspects of ownership have been explored by anthropologists, psychologists, social psychologists, geographers, philosophers, animal behaviorists, consumer behaviorists, historians, artists, and students of life-span development, among others. While ownership was generally experienced as involving person-object relations, it can also be felt toward non-physical entities such as ideas, words, artistic creations, and other people. Similarly, the sense of ownership that people develop towards their homes typically results in preoccupation with decoration. Home is often extolled in song, poetry, and proverb (Porteous, 1976).

Operational Definition

A sense of possession (feeling as though an object, entity, or idea is 'MINE' or 'OURS') is the core of psychological ownership (Furby, 1978). Possessive feelings are ubiquitous, can refer to tangible or intangible objects (Beaglehole, 1932; James, 1890), and can occur based on legal ownership or in that the possessive nature of psychological ownership for the organisation differentiates it from other work-related attitudes while simultaneously (and more importantly) allowing psychological ownership for the organisation to increase our understanding of employee attitudes and behavior, by explaining variance over and above existing constructs (such as commitment and satisfaction).

3.7   PERCEIVED ORGANISATIONAL SUPPORT

Conceptual Definition

Social exchange theories maintained that individuals enter into relationships with others to maximize their benefits (Blau, 1964; Homans, 1974). The resources exchanged between partners may be impersonal, that is, benefits whose value did not depend on the identity of the sender, for example, the provision of information or money (Foa & Foa, 1974). Resources may also be socio emotional, such as the communication of caring or respect. The norm of reciprocity, obligating the reciprocation of favorable treatment, serves as a starting mechanism for interpersonal relationships. Aid can be provided to another individual with the expectation that it will be paid back with resources desired by the donor (Gouldner, 1960). To that extent both partners possess and are willing to supply resources strongly desired by the other, reciprocation of increasingly valued resources strengthened the exchange relationship over time. Organisational support theory (OST: Eisenberger, Huntington, Hutchinson, & Sowa, 1986; Rhoades & Eisenberger, 2002; Shore & Shore, 1995) holds that in order to meet socio emotional needs and to assess the benefits of increased work effort, employees form a general perception concerning the extent to which the organisation values their contributions and cares about their well-being. Such perceived organisational support (POS) would increase employees felt obligation to help the organisation reach its objectives, their affective commitment to the organisation, and their expectation that improved performance would be rewarded. Behavioral outcomes of POS would include increase in in-role and extra-role performance and decrease in stress and withdrawal behaviors such as absenteeism and turnover.

Operational Definition

According to organisational support theory, the relationship between performance-reward expectancies and POS should be reciprocal (Eisenberger et al., 1986; Shore & Shore, 1995). Favorable opportunities for rewards would convey the organisation's positive valuation of employee's contributions and thus contribute to POS (C.F. Gaertner and Nollen, 1989). POS, In-turn, would increase employees expectancies that high performance will be rewarded.

Consistent with these views, the meta-analysis by Rhoades and Eisenberger (2002) found that opportunities for greater recognition, pay, and promotion were positively associated with POS. Additional research is needed concerning the mediating role of reward expectancies in the relationship between POS and performance.

3.8   INROLE PERFORMANCE

Conceptual Definition

Role theory had been used effectively by researchers in psychology, social psychology, sociology, organisation behavior, and human resource management since the early 1930s. Multiple researchers from these various fields have concluded that roles play an important part in social structure (Mead, 1934; Turner, 1978), and roles recognized as central to understand employee behavior in organisations (Katz & Kahn, 1978). According to identity theory, it was not the existence of roles, but their saliency, which affects behavior (Burke, 1991; Thoits, 1992). Identity theory suggests a process by which people use an internal control system to filter information. The likelihood that an event or information will trigger behavior is associated with the saliency of a particular role (Thoits, 1991; 1992).

When social structures are viewed as made up of roles, social stability is not explicable as a function of (a) the normative consensual commitment of individuals or (b) normative integration. Instead, dispenses and role strain-the difficulty of fulfilling role demands-are normal. In a sequence of role bargains, the individual's choices are shaped by mechanisms, outlined here, through which he organizes his total role system and performs well or ill in any role relationship.

Operational Definition

In-role performance is defined as the level of achievement at assigned job duties (Williams & Anderson, 1991).

3.9 PSYCHOLOGICAL WELL-BEING

Conceptual Definition

Bradburn's (1969) classic study, for example, gave little attention to the fundamental meaning of well-being. That positive and negative affect emerged as independent dimensions was, in fact, a serendipitous finding from a study conceived for other purposes. This theory distinguished between positive and negative affect and denned happiness as the balance between the two. Conceptual and methodological refinements built on this early operationalization of well-being. For example, the postulated independence of positive and negative affect was challenged and linked with the failure to distinguish between the intensity and the frequency of affect on one view; human beings always act in pursuit of what they think which will give them the greatest balance of pleasure over pain. What could be going on in ones mind would be related 'psychological hedonism', and reactions would often have an outcome like "will not be my concern here. Rather, I intend to discuss 'evaluative hedonism' or 'prudential hedonism', according to which well-being consists in the greatest balance of pleasure over pain".

Operational Definition

Adequate measurement of complex psychological states usually requires an iterative process; researchers must move several times between conceptualization and operationalization, adjusting their ideas and measures as they go. This is not always feasible within the span of a single research project, and it is sometimes necessary to accept or adapt a previously reported measure or to create a new scale with only limited opportunity for systematic development. Neither approach is entirely satisfactory, especially as most investigators have understandably given priority in their reports to substantive research questions rather than to the provision of detailed information about samples, means, variances, inter correlations and other features which would assist in subsequent assessment of their measures.

This problem is particularly evident in studies of the quality of working life and occupational well-being. The need to examine a large number of subjective variables has often led investigators to devise their own items or to select from previous measures small segments with unknown psychometric properties. An additional difficulty arises from the complexity and ill-defined scope of many concepts in the area; questionnaire items are sometimes difficult to comprehend, especially for blue-collar workers who are typically the focus of research. There is thus a need for development work to create robust instruments in the quality of working life area. Of particular value would be short scales which are easily completed by unsophisticated respondents, which are known to be psychometrically acceptable, and for which normative data are available. This paper contributes towards meeting this need by presenting eight separate scales for diagnostic and evaluative use in both research and practice. These measure work involvement, intrinsic job motivation, higher order need strength, perceived intrinsic job characteristics, job satisfaction, life satisfaction, happiness and self-rated anxiety.

- **Work Involvement** is viewed as the degree to which a person wants to be engaged in work.

- **Intrinsic Job Motivation** is viewed as the degree to which a person wants to work well in his or her job in order to achieve intrinsic satisfaction.

- **Higher Order Need Strength** is taken to be the importance which a person attaches to the attainment of higher order needs.

- **Perceived Intrinsic Job Characteristics** are the person's reports about the degree to which features are present in his or her job which might give rise to intrinsic satisfaction.

- **Job Satisfaction** is the degree to which a person reports satisfaction with intrinsic and extrinsic features of the job. Total job satisfaction is the sum of all separate items, and overall job satisfaction is reported satisfaction with the job as a whole.

- **Life Satisfaction** is the degree to which a person reports satisfaction with salient features of his life and life-space. Total life satisfaction is the sum of all separate items, and overall life satisfaction is reported satisfaction with one's life as a whole.

- **Happiness** is the degree to which a person reports that he or she is currently happy.

- **Self-rated Anxiety** is the degree to which a person reports anxiety about salient features of his or her life and life-space summed across items, and overall self-rated anxiety is reported anxiety in general.

3.10 ORGANISATIONAL COMMITMENT

Conceptual Definition

The term "commitment" enjoys an increasing vogue in sociological discussion. Sociologists use it in analyses of both individual and organisational behavior. They use it as a descriptive concept to mark out forms of action characteristic of particular kinds of people or groups. They used it as an independent variable to account for certain kinds of behavior of individuals and groups. They used it in analyses of a wide variety of phenomena such as power, religion, occupational recruitment, bureaucratic behavior, political behavior and so on. Organisational commitment revealed two major theoretical frameworks on which most studies were based. One is Homan's exchange theory (1958) according to which organisational commitment was seen as the outcome of the exchange relationship between the individual and the organisation. The theory suggested as the exchange becomes more favorable from the individual's point of view, his or her commitment to the organisation increases. The other theory (Becker, 1960) was an improvement on Homan's idea as, it introduces the element of time and the notion of side bets to the exchange paradigm. According to this theory organisational commitment appeared to be a structural phenomenon that occurs as a result of individual organisational transactions and alterations in side bets over time.

The concept of organisational commitment has grown in popularity and received a great deal of attention in the organisational behavior and industrial psychology literatures (Mathieu & Zajac, 1990. It was suggested that gaining a better understanding of the individual, group and organisational processes that were related to organisational commitment has significant implications for employees, organisations, and society (Conger, 1999; Koberg, Boss, Senjem, & Goodman, 1999, Mathieu & Zajac, 1990, Mowday, Porter & Steers, 1982; Potterfiel Janasz, & Quinn, 1999 in Zhu, et al, 2004).

Operational Definition

Meyer, Allen, & Smith (1993) say that the three types of commitment are a psychological state "that characterized the employee's relationship with the organisation or has the implications to affect whether the employee will continue with the organisation". Meyer et al (1993) continue to say that generally the research shows that those employee's with a strong affective commitment will remain with an organisation because they want to, those with a strong continuance commitment remain because they have to, and those with a normative commitment remain because they felt that they have to. Meyer & Allen (1997) define a committed employee as being one "stay with an organisation, attends work regularly, puts in a full day and more protected corporate assets, and believes in the organisational goals". This employee positively contributes to the organisation because of its commitment to the organisation.

Affective Commitment is defined as the emotional attachment, identification, and involvement that an employee has with its organisation and goals (Mowday et al, 1997, Meyer & Allen, 1993; O'Reily & Chatman). Porter et al (1974) further characterize affective commitment by three factors (1) "belief in and acceptance of the organisation's goals and values, (2) a willingness to focus effort on helping the organisation achieve its goals and (3) a desire to maintain organisational membership". Mowday et al (1979) further state that affective communication is "when the employee identifies with a particular organisation and its goals in order to maintain membership to facilitate the goal". Meyer and Allen (1997) continue to say that employees retain membership out of choice and this is their commitment to the organisation.

Continuance Commitment is the willingness to remain in an organisation because of the investment that the employee has with "nontransferable" investments. Nontransferable investments include things such as retirement, relationships with other employees, or things that are special to the organisation (Reichers, 1985). Continuance commitment also includes factors such as years of employment or benefits that the employee may receive that are unique to the organisation (Reichers, 1985). Meyer and Allen (1997) further explain that employees who share continuance commitment with their employer often make it very difficult for an employee to leave the organisation.

Normative Commitment is the commitment that a person believes that they have to the organisation or their feeling of obligation to their workplace (Bolon, 1993). In 1982, Weiner discusses normative commitment as being a "generalized value of loyalty and duty". Meyer and Allen (1991) supported this type of commitment prior to Bolon's definition, with their definition of normative commitment being "a feeling of obligation". It is argued that normative commitment is only natural due to the way we are raised in society. Normative commitment can be explained by other commitments such as marriage, family, religion, etc. Therefore when it comes to one's commitment to their place of employment they often feel like they have a moral obligation to the organisation (Wiener, 1982).

3.11 ORGANISATIONAL CITIZENSHIP BEHAVIOR

Conceptual Definition

Chester Barnard's concept (Barnard, 1938) of the "willingness to cooperate", and "Social Exchange Theory" - Blau (1964) was among the first to differentiate social exchange from economic exchange. According to Blau, social exchange refers to relationships that entail unspecified future obligations. Like economic exchange, social exchange generates an expectation of some future return for contributions; however, unlike economic exchange, the exact nature of that return is unspecified. Furthermore, social exchange does not occur on a quid pro quo or calculated basis.

Economic exchange is based on transactions, but social exchange relationships are based on individuals' trusting that the other parties to the exchanges will fairly discharge their obligations in the long run (Holmes, 1981) were the basic models which helps in development of the new concept Organisational citizenship behavior. Katz (1964) identified three categories of employee behavior essential for organisational effectiveness. According to Katz, individuals must first be induced to enter and remain with an organisation; as employees, they must carry out specific role requirements in a dependable fashion; and they must engage in innovative and spontaneous activity that goes beyond role prescriptions. Organ (1988) proposed that supervisor fairness leads to employee citizenship because a social exchange relationship develops between employees and their supervisors.

Operational Definition

An organisational citizenship behavior is defined as an "individual behavior that is discretionary, not directly or explicitly recognized by the formal reward system, and that in the aggregate promotes the effective functioning of the organisation Organ (1988). By discretionary, we mean that the behavior is not an enforceable requirement of the role or the job description, that is, the clearly specifiable terms of the person's employment contract with the organisation; the behavior is rather a matter of personal choice, such that its omission is not generally understood as punishable. The following are the essential requirements for the superior-subordinate behavior in the organisation.

Civic Virtue is defined as subordinate participation in organisation political life and supporting the administrative function of the organisation (Deluga, 1998). It is referring to the responsibility of the subordinates to participate in the life of the firm such as attending meetings which are not required by the firm and keeping up with the changes in the organisation (Organ, 1988). This dimension of OCB is actually derived from Graham's findings which stated that employees should have the responsibility to be a good citizen of the organisation (Graham, 1991). These behaviors reflect an employees recognition of being part of organisation and accept the responsibilities which entails (Podsakoff et al., 2000). Other researchers have found that civic virtue enhances the quantity of performance and help to reduce customer complaints (Walz & Niehoff, 1996).

Conscientiousness is used to indicate that a particular individual is organized, accountable and hardworking. Organ (1988) defined it as dedication to the job which exceed formal requirements such as working for long hours, and volunteer to perform jobs besides duties. In addition to that, studies have also revealed that conscientiousness can be related to organisational politics among employees (McCrae & Costa, 1987). Kidder and McLean Parks (1993) posited the fact that males are more likely to engage in conscientious behavior than females in view of the fact that males has preference for equity over equality.

Altruism involves voluntary behaviors where an employee provides assistance to an individual with a particular problem to complete his or her task under unusual circumstances Smith, Organ and Near (1983). Altruism refers to a member helping other members of the organisation in their work. Podsakoff et al. (2000) has demonstrated that altruism was significantly related to performance evaluations and correspondingly, positive affectivity.

Courtesy includes behaviors, which focus on the prevention of problems and taking the necessary step so as to lessen the effects of the problem in the future. In other words, courtesy means a member encourages other workers when they are demoralized and feel discouraged about their professional development. Early research efforts have found that employees who exhibit courtesy would reduce intergroup conflict and thereby diminishes the time spent on conflict management activities (Podsakoff et al., 2000).

Sportsmanship is the behavior of warmly tolerating the irritations that are an unavoidable part of nearly every organisational setting Organ (1988). Podsakoff and MacKenzie (1997) revealed that good sportsmanship would enhance the morale of the work group and subsequently reduce employee turnover.

3.12   INDEPENDENT AND DEPENDENT VARIABLE:

Based on Bernard and Simon (Theory of Organisational Equilibrium) and Bernard (Theory of Formal Organisation) following dimensions of ERM were identified as Independent variable.

1. Psychological contract and its dimensions such as loyalty, specific, stability, external marketability, employee development, performance support, mistrust, erosion, uncertainty, employee fulfilment and employer fulfilment.

2. Psychological empowerment and its dimensions such as meaning, competence, self-determination and impact.

3. Employee involvement and its dimension such as information, knowledge, reward and power.

4. Cultural intelligence and its dimensions such as metacognitive, cognitive, motivational and behavioural.

5. Perceived organisational support

6. Psychological ownership

7. Inrole performance.

On the basis of literature review and assumption of Bernard and Simon (Theory of Organisational Equilibrium) and Bernard (Theory of Formal Organisation) theories, following dimensions of psychological well-being, organisational commitment and organisational citizenship behavior were identified as Dependent variable.

1. Psychological well-being consist of work involvement, perceived intrinsic job motivation, high order need strength, perceived job characteristics, job satisfaction, life satisfaction, happiness and self-anxiety.

2. Organisational commitment includes affective commitment, continuance commitment and normative commitment.

3. Organisational citizenship behavior measured through altruism, conscientiousness, civic virtue, courtesy and sportsmanship.

3.13   CONCEPTUAL FRAMEWORK OF THE STUDY

Most of the research focused mainly on performance and well-being of employee in an organisation. With a view to diversify the research, the author conducted a study to explore the relationship between Managers and Employees perception regarding ERM factors towards employee well being, their level of commitment and also their behavior at work place. Based on the above discussion the conceptual model was developed to understand the various factors influencing public sector bank employee and managers relationship. This model helps both manager and employees to understand each other perception. The following diagram represents the conceptual model of ERM.

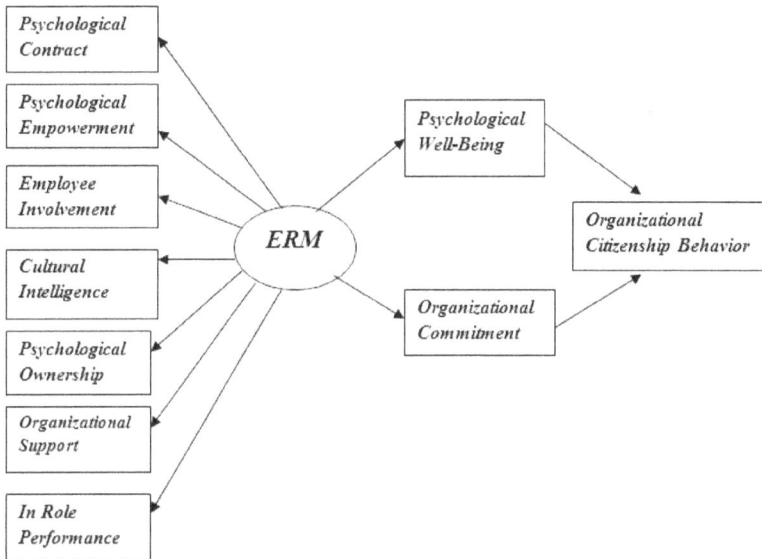

Figure 3.1   Conceptual Framework of the Study

Summarizing the results it is identified that ERM dimensions have positive effect on individual well-being and their work place behavior. The main purpose of this study was to examine the relationship between comprehensive set of ERM variables towards individual wellbeing and their work place behavior. The above framework enlighten that ERM has a positive impact on the psychological wellbeing, organisational commitment and organisational citizenship behavior. Independent and dependent variables identified through these theories are to be analyzed.

4

ANALYTICAL DETAILS AND DISCUSSIONS ON ERM

4.1 INTRODUCTION

Various research scales to measure Employee Relationship Management and suggestions for improving the relationship are included in this chapter. This chapter provides the analytical details and discussions of the study conducted by the author. Analysis and interpretation play a vital role in good research. The aim of the analysis is to arrange, organise and précis the collected data in order to understand and give answers for the research questions. Analysis of research cannot be fulfilled without presenting the results in a proper way i.e., interpretation; therefore, analysis and interpretation in a research are interdependent.

A detailed analysis for the collected data was performed. ANOVA and t- test were used to examine research hypotheses and based on findings of the study, interpretations and conclusions were drawn. Descriptive analysis and inferential statistics through Statistical Packages for Social Science 16 (SPSS 16) were used to analyze the data.

4.2 DESCRIPTIVE ANALYSIS ON SAMPLE

Frequency and Percentage analysis was one of the popular statistical measures used to describe the characteristics of the sample or population in totality.

4.2.0 DEMOGRAPHIC PROFILE OF THE EMPLOYEES AND MANAGERS WORKING IN PUBLIC SECTOR BANKS

The demographic profile of the respondents had been understood by several variables such as Gender, Age, Level of Education, Marital Status, Annual income and their Work experience in their banks. Based on the questionnaire response, their personal and occupational details were analyzed and results are presented below.

4.2.1   Employees Demographic Details

4.2.1.1 *Frequency distribution of gender*

Table 4.2.1.1   Gender of the Employees

Gender	Frequency	Percent
Male	117	46.8
Female	133	53.2
Total	250	100.0

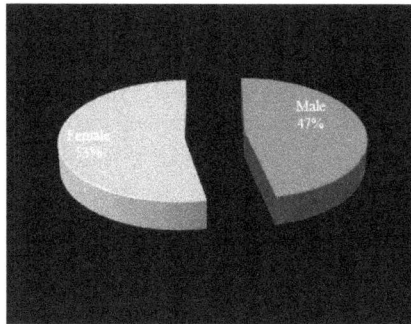

Figure 4.2.1.1   Pie Chart Shows the Gender Composition

The above table reveals that 47% respondents of this study belonged to male and 53% respondents of this study belonged to female.

4.2.1.2 *Marital status of the respondents*

Table 4.2.1.2   Marital Status of Employees

Marital Status	Frequency	Percent
Married	198	79.2
Unmarried	52	20.8
Total	250	100.0

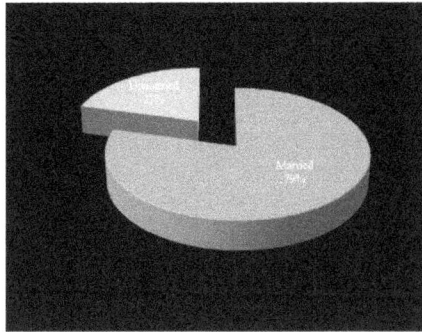

Figure 4.2.1.2 Pie Chart shows the Marital Status of Employees.

The above table reveals that 79.2% of respondents of this study were married and 20.8% respondents were unmarried. Therefore majority of respondents were married.

4.2.1.3 *Educational level of the respondents*

Table 4.2.1.3 Levels of Education of Employees.

Educational Qualification	Frequency	Percent
Under Graduate	144	57.6
Post Graduate	88	35.2
Others	18	7.2
Total	250	100.0

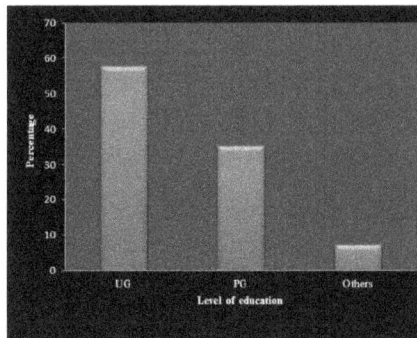

Figure 4.2.1.3 Bar Chart shows the Educational Qualification of Employees.

The above table reveals that 57.6% respondents were graduates, 35.2% respondents were post graduates and 7.2% respondents belonged to other category. Other categories include ITI, C.A (IIB), B.Tech.

4.2.1.4 *Annual salary details of the respondents*

Table 4.2.1.4   Annual Salary of Employees

Annual Salary in Lakhs	Frequency	Percent
Up to 3	82	32.8
3 – 5	85	34.0
5 -7	76	30.4
Above 7	7	2.8
Total	250	100.0

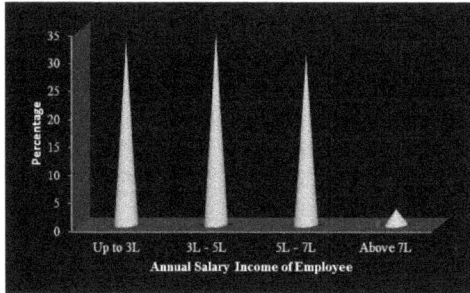

Figure 4.2.1.4   Cone Chart shows the Annual Salary of Employees

The above table reveals that 32.8% respondents are earning up to Rs 3lakhs p.a., 34% respondents earning between 3-5lakhs, 30.4% respondents are earning between 5-7lakhs, 2.8% respondents are earning Above 7lakhs. Therefore majority of respondents were earning 3 to 5lakhs as their annual salary.

4.2.1.5 *Age distribution of the respondents*

Table 4.2.1.5   Age Distribution of Employees

Age Group in years	Frequency	Percent
Up to 30	80	32.0
31-40	37	14.8

Age Group in years	Frequency	Percent
41-50	55	22.0
Above 50	78	31.2
Total	250	100.0

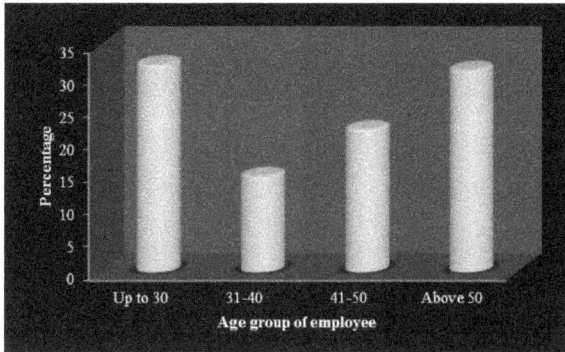

Figure 4.2.1.5 Cylindrical Chart shows the Age Group of Employees.

The above table reveals that 32% respondents belonged to up to 30 years of age, 14.8% respondents belonged to 31-40 yrs of age, 22% respondents belonged to 41-50 yrs of age and 31.2% respondents belonged to above 50yrs of age. Therefore maximum numbers of respondents were youngsters i.e. their age is up to 30years

4.2.1.6 *Work experience of the respondents*

Table 4.2.1.6 Work Experience of Employees.

Work experience in years	Frequency	Percent
Up to 10	86	34.4
11- 20	43	17.2
21 - 30	68	27.2
Above 31	53	21.2
Total	250	100.0

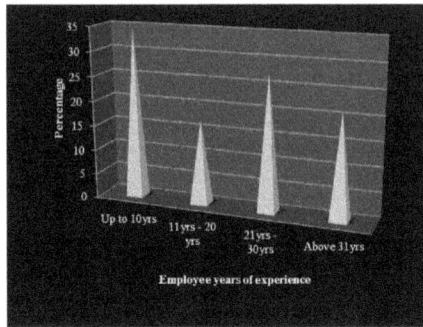

Figure 4.2.1.6 Pyramid Chart shows the Work Experience of Employees.

The above table reveals that 34.4% respondents had up to 10yrs of experience, 17.2% respondents were between 11-20yrs of experience, 27.2% respondents were between 21-30yrs of experience and 21.2% respondents were having above 31 years of experience.

4.2.2. Manager Demographic Details

Gender of the respondent

Table 4.2.2.1 Gender of the Managers.

Gender	Frequency	Percent
Male	96	83.5
Female	19	16.5
Total	115	100.0

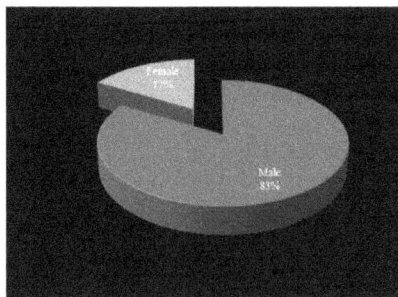

Figure 4.2.2.1 Pie Chart shows the Gender Composition of Managers.

The above table reveals that 83.5% respondents of this study belonged to male and 16.5% respondents of this study belonged to female. Therefore more male respondents were in manager grade and more female respondents were employee grade.

4.2.2.2 *Marital Status of the respondents*

Table 4.2.2.2 Marital Status of the Managers.

Marital Status	Frequency	Percent
Married	107	93.0
Unmarried	8	7.0
Total	115	100.0

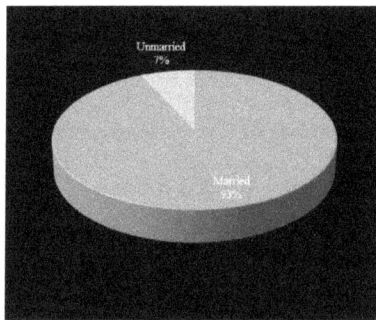

Figure 4.2.2.2 Pie Chart shows the Marital Status of Managers.

The above table reveals that 93% respondents of this study were married and 7% respondents were unmarried. Therefore maximum respondents are married.

4.2.2.3 *Educational level of the respondents*

Table 4.2.2.3 Educational Level of Managers.

Educational Qualification	Frequency	Percent
UG	69	60.0
PG	39	33.9
Others	7	6.1
Total	115	100.0

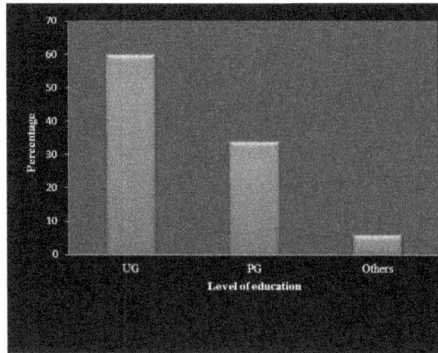

Figure 4.2.2.3   Bar Chart shows the Educational Qualification of Managers.

The above table reveals that 60% respondents were graduates, 33.9% respondents were post graduates and 6.1% respondents belonged to other category like ITI, C.A (IIB) B.Tech.

4.2.2.4 *Annual salary details of the respondents*

Table 4.2.10   Annual Salary of Managers

Annual Salary in Lakhs	Frequency	Percent
3L – 5L	16	13.9
5L -7L	44	38.3
Above 7L	55	47.8
Total	115	100.0

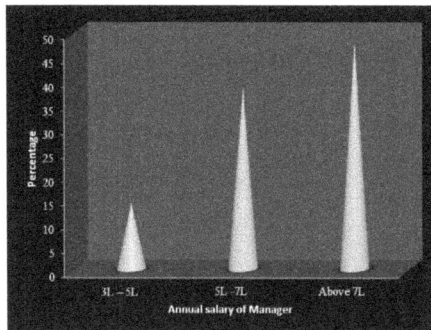

Figure 4.2.2.4   Cone Chart shows the Annual Salary of Managers.

The above table reveals that 13.9% respondents are earning between 3-5lakhs, 38.3% respondents are earned between 5-7lakhs and 47.8% respondents earned above 7lakhs. Therefore maximum number of managers were earning above 7lakhs.

4.2.2.5 *Age distribution of the respondents*

Table 4.2.2.5   Age Distribution Of Managers.

Age Group in years	Frequency	Percent
Up to 30	5	4.3
31-40	15	13.0
41-50	20	17.4
Above 50	75	65.2
Total	115	100.0

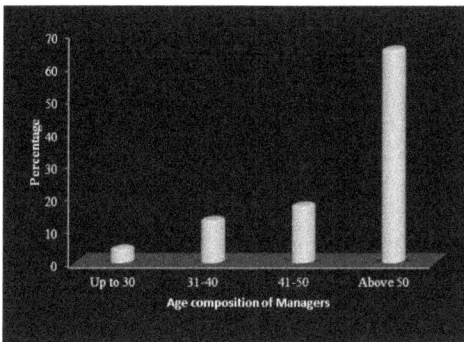

Figure 4.2.2.5 Cylindrical Chart shows the Age Distribution of Managers.

The above table reveals that 4.3% respondents belonged to less than 30 yrs of age, 13% respondents belonged to 31-40 yrs of age, 17.4% respondents belonged to 41-50 yrs of age and 65.2% respondents belonged to above 50yrs age. Therefore maximum numbers of respondents were above 50yrs of age.

4.2.2.6 *Work experience of the respondents*

Table 4.2.2.6   Work Experience of Managers.

Work experience in years	Frequency	Percent
Up to 10yrs	8	7.0
11yrs – 20yrs	15	13.0
21yrs - 30 yrs	35	30.4
Above 31yrs	57	49.6
Total	115	100.0

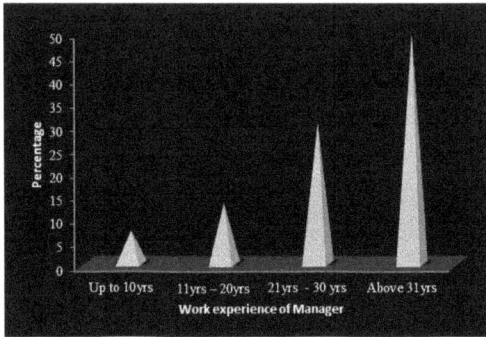

Figure 4.2.2.6   Pyramid Chart shows the Work Experience of Managers.

The above table reveals that 7% respondents were having up to 10yrs of experience, 13% respondents were between 11-20yrs of experience, 30.4% respondents were between 21-30yrs of experience, and 49.6% respondents were having above 31 years of experience. Therefore maximum numbers of manager were having more than 31 years of experience.

4.2.3   Level of Employment of the Respondents

Table 4.2.3   Level of Employment of the Respondents.

Designations	Frequency	Percent
Manager	115	31.5
Employees	250	68.5
Total	365	100.0

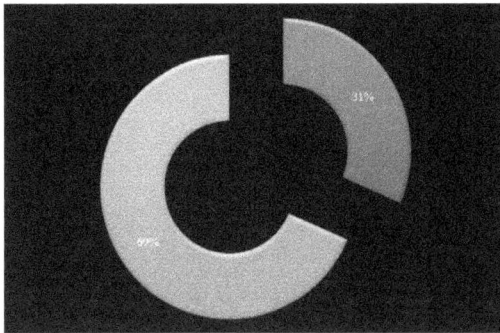

Figure 4.2.3 Dough Nut Chart shows Employee and Manager Respondents.

The above table shows that data were collected from managers 115 (31%) and employees 250 (69%) working in public sector banks.

4.2.4 Work Place Socialising

Collaboration starts from the aspect of relating well to others. Socialising is an important factor as employees spend close to 12 hours in the organisation. It is important to understand the friendship circle and how each employee influences one another to get a critical task done.

Table 4.2.4 Socialising – 1

SOC 1	MANAGER		EMPLOYEE	
	Frequency	Percent	Frequency	Percent
Yes	108	93.9	242	96.8
No	7	6.1	8	3.2
Total	115	100.0	250	100.0

More than 90% of both employees and managers feel that they need friends at their work place.

4.2.5 Importance of Socialising

The employees were asked about the importance of socializing at work place and how it enhances the atmosphere. The results are presented in the following table.

Table 4.2.5   Socialising – 2

SOC 2	MANAGER		EMPLOYEE	
	Frequency	Percent	Frequency	Percent
Yes	104	90.4	231	92.4
No	11	9.6	19	7.6
Total	115	100.0	250	100.0

The table reveals more than 90% of both employees and managers feel that socialising at their work place is very much important to achieve their task easily.

4.2.6   Role of Networking

Managers and employees were asked about the networking and its requirement. The need for socialising is presented in the following table.

Table 4.2.6   Socialising – 3

SOC 3	MANAGER		EMPLOYEE	
	Frequency	Percent	Frequency	Percent
Yes	104	90.4	185	74.0
No	11	9.6	65	26.0
Total	115	100.0	250	100.0

The table reveals 90% of managers think that networking is very much essential to expand their business, but this is not in the case of employees, only 74% of employees feel that they need networking with larger organisation in order to expand the business.

4.2.7   Sharing Personal Issues

Employees spend most of their waking hours at office on an average of 12 hours. The respondents were asked about the factor that binds employees/managers not just at a professional front but also on the personal front. The following table presents the extent of relationship.

Table 4.2.7   Socialising – 4

SOC 4	MANAGER		EMPLOYEE	
	Frequency	Percent	Frequency	Percent
Yes	63	54.8	158	63.2
No	52	45.2	92	36.8
Total	115	100.0	250	100.0

From the above table one can find out that around 55% of Managers discuss their personal inconvenience with his/her friend; almost 63% of employees discuss their personal issue with their friends, which in-turn might help them to find solution for their personal issues.

4.2.8   Job Contentment

This is to gauge the happiness quotient of the employees in their current role. Contentment with the job is important as it is a major driving force towards performance. The extent of job contentment is presented in the following table.

Table 4.2.8   Happiness – 1

Happiness - 1	MANAGER		EMPLOYEE	
	Frequency	Percent	Frequency	Percent
Yes	103	89.6	225	90.0
No	12	10.4	25	10.0
Total	115	100.0	250	100.0

The above table reveals 90% of employees and managers working in the public sector banks feel happy about the current employment. It seems that their obligations were met by each other.

4.2.9   Job Delights

In this question an understanding is sought on the happiness quotient that goes beyond job satisfaction. Many organisation wish to retain their employees, one of the factors to retain them is their love towards the job. The respondents were asked about their level of happiness towards their present job and it is presented below.

Table 4.2.9   Happiness – 2

Happiness – 2	MANAGER		EMPLOYEE	
	Frequency	Percent	Frequency	Percent
Yes	103	89.6	224	89.6
No	12	10.4	26	10.4
Total	115	100.0	250	100.0

The above table reveals that nearly 90% of employees and manager expressed happiness about their job. This is heartening to note and surely reflect on the productivity and quality of work.

4.2.10   Work Satisfaction

This question was raised to understand the employees and managers satisfaction towards growth opportunity in their current position.

Table 4.2.10   Satisfaction - 1

SAT 1	MANAGER		EMPLOYEE	
	Frequency	Percent	Frequency	Percent
Yes	96	83.5	206	82.4
No	19	16.5	44	17.6
Total	115	100.0	250	100.0

The above table reveals that 96% of managers were satisfied with the growth opportunity in their job whereas only 82% of employees were satisfied with the growth opportunity.

4.2.11   Life Satisfaction

Life satisfaction is an important factor that motivates employees/ employers to move from home to work and vice-versa. In this question an understanding is sought on the employees and managers satisfaction towards their life.

Table 4.2.11   Satisfaction – 2

SAT 4	MANAGER		EMPLOYEE	
	Frequency	Percent	Frequency	Percent
Yes	85	73.9	187	74.8
No	30	26.1	63	25.2
Total	115	100.0	250	100.0

The above table reveals that 85% of managers working in the public sector banks accepted that they were living their comfortable life whereas only 75% of employees working in the public sector banks lead a comfortable life.

4.2.12   Training & Development

Training is integral part of an organisation. This helps in updating the skills and equips employees to face the changing environment. Repetitive work will only make employer/employee to avoid looking beyond the current role. Respondents were asked about the training opportunity present and their views are presented in the following table.

Table 4.2.12   Training & Development

T & D	MANAGER		EMPLOYEE	
	Frequency	Percent	Frequency	Percent
Yes	109	94.8	235	94.0
No	6	5.2	15	6.0
Total	115	100.0	250	100.0

The above table reveals that almost 94% of both employees and managers working in the public sector bank accepted that they were receiving appropriate training from the organisation to perform their duties efficiently.

4.2.13   Job Turnover

In this question an understanding is sought if an employee/employer when given a chance would look at other opportunities within and outside the organisation.

Table 4.2.13   Turnover

Turnover	MANAGER		EMPLOYEE	
	Frequency	Percent	Frequency	Percent
Yes	17	14.8	59	23.6
No	98	85.2	191	76.4
Total	115	100.0	250	100.0

The above table reveals that 85% of managers working in the public sector banks were not having an idea to quit their job; likewise 76% of employees were not ready to quit their job. This shows that they were very much satisfied with their job.

4.2.14   Work Life Balance

It is quite natural to think about the job at odd time due to job pressure. The employees and managers working in the public sector banks were asked whether they think about their job even when they were not actually involved in the work. Their state of mind is presented in the following table.

Table 4.2.14   Work Life Balance (WLB) – 1

WLB1	MANAGER		EMPLOYEE	
	Frequency	Percent	Frequency	Percent
ALWAYS	8	7.0	21	8.4
OFTEN	34	29.6	22	8.8
SOMETIMES	35	30.4	108	43.2
RARELY	26	22.6	69	27.6
NEVER	12	10.4	30	12.0
Total	115	100.0	250	100.0

The above table reveals that nearly 30% of managers were often thought about their job even though they were not actually at work but this was not the situation in case of employees but almost 43% of employees sometimes think about their work even though they were out of the work.

4.2.15 Job Fulfillment

One of the important factors that boost morale among employees is how they think their time at work is spent. The happier they are at work is reflected in their performance. Following table present the feeling at work.

Table 4.2.15 Work Life Balance (WLB) – 2

WLB 2	MANAGER		EMPLOYEE	
	Frequency	Percent	Frequency	Percent
VERY UNHAPPY	6	5.2	7	2.8
UNHAPPY	8	7.0	23	9.2
INDIFFERENT	10	8.7	25	10.0
HAPPY	75	65.2	159	63.6
VERY HAPPY	16	13.9	36	14.4
Total	115	100.0	250	100.0

From the above table, maximum number of managers as well as employees feels happy in spending their time at work.

4.2.16 Work Stress

The respondents were asked about the intensity of work and how it has affected them physically and mentally. Work pressure and schedules take a tole on health. The level of stress experienced by the respondents is presented in the following table.

Table 4.2.16 Work Life Balance (WLB) – 3

WLB 3	MANAGER		EMPLOYEE	
	Frequency	Percent	Frequency	Percent
ALWAYS	2	1.7	9	3.6
OFTEN	9	7.8	17	6.8
SOMETIMES	47	40.9	98	39.2

WLB 3	MANAGER		EMPLOYEE	
	Frequency	Percent	Frequency	Percent
RARELY	33	28.7	83	33.2
NEVER	24	20.9	43	17.2
Total	115	100.0	250	100.0

From the above table, nearly 40% of both employees and managers working in the public sector banks sometimes feel depressed because of their extensive work pressure. Approximately 10% of both managers and employees often feel depressed because of their work.

4.3   INFERENTIAL ANALYSIS ON SAMPLE

Normality had been tested to find the sample population represents total population; Reliability analysis was used to measure the reliable percentage of collected data.

Difference between two groups in the mean scores of variables is studied using Independent sample t test and are discussed in this section.

Further, to analyze the variation among the group ANOVA has been used and also Chi-square test was performed to know the association between the variables.

Factor analysis was conducted in order to identify the most influencing factors of ERM between employees and managers.

Multiple regression analysis was conducted to examine the relationship between the ERM dimensions and Psychological well-being, Organisational Commitment and Organisational Citizenship Behavior.

Discriminant analysis was used to predict a categorical dependent variable. In this study categorical dependent variable is work position i.e., designation (Employees/ Managers).

4.3.1   TEST OF NORMALITY

To analyze the factors influencing the relationship between employees and managers working in the public sector banks, psychological contract, psychological empowerment, employee involvement, cultural intelligence, psychological ownership, perceived organisational support and in role performance were considered as ERM dimensions; PW, OC and OCB were also taken. In order to find whether sample population represent the total population Normality test was performed.

Hypotheses: The Sample Population Of The Study Represents The Total Population

Table 4.3.1 Normality Test to Represent the Population

Variables	Kolmogorov- Smirnov Z	Asymp. Sig. (2-tailed)
Psychological contract	1.00	0.27
Psychological Empowerment	1.11	0.17
Involvement	1.23	0.09
Cultural Intelligence	1.29	0.07
Psychological ownership	1.18	0.12
Organisational support	1.09	0.19
In role performance	1.30	0.07
Psychological wellbeing	1.00	0.27
Commitment	1.09	0.18
Organisational citizenship behavior	1.09	0.18

Since p value in all ERM dimension and also PW, OC and OCB is greater than 0.05 therefore null hypotheses is accepted; hence the sample population (Employee n_1 = 250, Managers n_2 = 115) represent the opinion of the total population.

4.3.2 RELIABILITY

Reliability refers to the quality of a measurement procedure that provides repeatability and accuracy. The Cronbach Reliability scores of the dimensions selected for the study is presented in the following table.

Table 4.3.2   Results of Reliability Analysis

S.No	Variables	Reliability Analysis		No. of Items	
		Employee	Manager	Employee	Manager
1.	Psychological contract	.908	.866	40	40
	1. Loyalty	.875	.664	4	4
	2. Specific	.621	.855	4	4
	3. Performance support	.860	.899	4	4
	4. Employee development	.905	.815	4	4
	5. Marketability	.749	.842	4	4
	6. Stability	.792	.898	4	4
	7. No trust	.784	.710	4	4
	8. Uncertainty	.926	.909	4	4
	9. Erosion	.859	.881	4	4
	10. Employee fulfillment	.678	.884	2	2
	11. Employer fulfillment	.828	.921	2	2
2.	Psychological Empowerment	.796	.866	12	12
	1. Meaning	.872	.808	3	3
	2. Competence	.679	.694	3	3
	3. Self Determination	.692	.708	3	3
	4. Impact	.828	.822	3	3
3.	Psychological wellbeing	.927	.937	55	56
	1. Job Satisfaction	.871	.888	14	15
	2. Work Involvement	.580	.396	4	4

S.No	Variables	Reliability Analysis		No. of Items	
		Employee	Manager	Employee	Manager
	3. Intrinsic Job Motivation	.817	.841	6	6
	4. High Order Need	.818	.781	6	6
	5. Perceived Intrinsic Job Characteristic	.866	.819	8	8
	6. Life Satisfaction	.802	.647	10	10
	7. Happiness			1	1
	8. Self Anxiety	.705	.712	6	6
4.	Commitment	.777	.819	18	18
	1. Affective commitment	.781	.842	6	6
	2. Continuance Commitment	.586	.729	6	6
	3. Normative commitment	.747	.664	6	6
5.	Involvement	.906	.926	13	13
	1. Information	.769	.812	4	4
	2. Reward	.775	.881	3	3
	3. Knowledge	.780	.834	3	3
	4. Power	.857	.819	3	3
6.	Cultural Intelligence	.913	.948	20	20
	1. Meta cognitive	.887	.900	4	4
	2. Cognitive	.887	.919	6	6
	3. Motivational	.863	.849	5	5
	4. Behavioral	.880	.887	5	5
7.	Psychological ownership	.835	.864	7	7
8.	Organisational support	.722	.769	8	8

S.No	Variables	Reliability Analysis		No. of Items	
		Employee	Manager	Employee	Manager
9.	In role performance	.688	.514	7	7
10.	Organisational citizenship behavior	.843	.824	25	25
	1. Altruism	.791	.797	5	5
	2. Conscientiousness	.666	.598	5	5
	3. Courtesy	.750	.821	5	5
	4. Civic Virtue	.543	.564	5	5
	5. Sportsmanship	.699	.720	5	5
Over all		.966	.971	205	206

Cronbach's Alpha is greater than 0.50 in all dimensions and sub dimensions of ERM, PW, OC and OCB, further for over all dimensions it is 0.966 i.e., 96.6% of collected data were reliable. Therefore it is statically proved that the data collected for the study is more reliable and these data were considered for further analysis.

4.3.3 TO IDENTIFY THE DIFFERENCES BETWEEN EMPLOYEE AND MANAGER WITH REGARDS TO ERM DIMENSIONS AND PSYCHOLOGICAL WELL-BEING, ORGANISATIONAL COMMITMENT AND ORGANISATIONAL CITIZENSHIP BEHAVIOR

Hypotheses - 1

Null Hypotheses: There is no significant difference between work position and ERM dimensions.

Table 4.3.3   T Test Employee Relationship Management (ERM)

ERM Dimensions	Designation				T value	P value
	Manager		Employees			
	Mean	SD	Mean	SD		
Psychological contract	151.89	13.74	139.27	18.32	6.579	<0.000

ERM Dimensions	Designation				T value	P value
	Manager		Employees			
	Mean	SD	Mean	SD		
Psychological Empowerment	49.23	5.16	46.12	5.67	5.003	<0.000
Involvement	48.70	7.77	45.67	8.32	3.302	0.001**
Cultural Intelligence	73.50	11.32	69.48	12.55	2.923	.004**
Psychological ownership	30.16	4.75	27.66	4.87	4.592	<0.000
Organisational support	29.31	4.57	27.49	5.05	3.304	0.001**
In role performance	27.20	3.28	25.73	3.74	3.629	<0.000

** Denotes significant at 1% level.

Since P value is less than 0.01 in all dimensions of ERM, the null hypothesis is rejected at 1 percent level of significance. Hence it is concluded that there is significant difference between ERM perception of employees and managers working in the public sector banks.

4.3.3.1 *To examine the employer-employee relationship through Psychological Contract*

Psychological contract is an unwritten mutual contract between employer and employee at the time of hiring. For research purpose branch manager of bank were considered as an agent of the employer and the employees view the agent as the employer. For this purpose the psychological contract is classified as –

1. Obligation of employee and employer – Employee is obligated to remain with the bank and support the organisation. Likewise manager is committed to support the well-being and interests of employees and their families. Loyalty, specific, dynamic performance, employee development, marketability, stability were considered as the dimensions of ER-EE Obligation.

2. Psychological contract transition – it measures Breach of contract i.e., Mistrust, Uncertainty and Erosion

3. Fulfillment of employer and employee – it measures commitment and fulfillment of managers and employees.

In order to find out the difference of option about psychological contract between manager and employee and also to find the relationship between employees and manager working in the public sector bank, Independent t test was performed.

Independent t test helps to measure the significant differences between managers and employees perception towards psychological contract and also these differences help to analyze employment relationship between managers and employees.

Hypotheses – 1.1

Null Hypotheses: There is no significant difference between work position and Psychological Contract Dimensions.

Table 4.3.3.1   T Test for Psychological Contract

Psychological Contract Dimensions	Manager		Employee		T value	P value
	Mean	SD	Mean	SD		
Loyalty	16.65	1.96	13.62	3.46	8.755	<0.000
Specific	14.80	3.13	11.95	3.06	8.214	<0.000
Dynamic performance	17.18	1.91	14.49	3.29	8.163	<0.000
Employee development	16.97	1.86	15.69	3.01	4.212	<0.000
Marketability	11.90	3.68	13.03	3.07	3.057	0.002**
Stability	16.29	3.03	17.03	2.23	2.624	0.009**
No trust	14.83	2.64	13.26	3.15	4.665	<0.000
Un certainty	14.23	3.30	13.26	3.59	2.460	0.014*
Erosion	13.23	3.79	12.60	3.81	1.469	0.143

Psychological Contract Dimensions	Designation				T value	P value
	Manager		Employee			
	Mean	SD	Mean	SD		
Employee fulfillment	8.16	1.23	7.34	1.51	5.052	<0.000
Employer fulfillment	7.64	1.36	7.00	1.71	3.524	<0.000
Overall Psychological contract	151.89	13.74	139.27	18.32	6.579	<0.000

** Denotes significant at 1% level. 2. * Denotes significant at 5% level

Loyalty is considered to be an important factor across any relations. It may be either organisation – client, banker – customer or employer – employee relations. Employee obligated to perform his duty through which he/she manifest loyalty, in-turn their managers committed themselves to help those employees and gave his/her constant support and interest towards employee well-being. From the above table, it can be concluded at 1% level of significance that there is a significant difference between the managers and employees towards loyalty (t = 8.755, p = 0.000). Hence, managers working in the public sector banks were more loyal compared to their employees.

Specific is nothing but the limited set of duties assigned to employees for what they agreed to pay. Employer provides only limited or little training to employees to perform their task. It is proved at 1% level of significance that there is a significant difference between the managers and employees specific (t = 8.214, p = 0.000). It can be further concluded at 1% level of significance that there is a significant difference between employees and managers perception towards their specific. Therefore managers provide the adequate training to their employees in order to perform their duties efficiently. But employees feel there is a scope for training.

Employee is obligated to successfully perform new and more demanding goals, which can change again and again in the future, to help the firm become and remain competitive. Employer has committed to promote continuous learning and to help employees successfully execute escalating performance requirements. There is a significant difference between the managers and employees perception towards dynamic performance ($t = 8.163$, $p = 0.000$) at 1% level of significance. Hence, managers working in the public sector banks were able to more actively perform their work.

Developmental opportunities in an organisation motivate the employees to trust their manager. One of the main duties a manager does is employee's performance evaluation and generates a developmental plan for employee's career advancement. There is a significant difference between employees and managers perception towards their developmental opportunity ($t = 4.212$, $p = 0.000$) at 1% level of significance. But manager's working in the public sector banks were creating the good career development opportunities to their employees within the bank.

Employees try to expand their external network for their career development and to improve their marketable skill. There is a significant difference between the managers and employees perception towards marketability ($t = 3.057$, $p = 0.002$) at 1% level of significance. Compared to managers, employees working in public sector banks have more external network (outside and within the bank) for their career development.

Stability means the willingness to continue with the bank to perform their duties. For this purpose it is the duty of the employer to provide stable income for the employment. It can be concluded at 1% level of significance that there is a significant difference between the managers and employees perception towards stability ($t = 2.642$, $p = 0.009$). Compared to managers, employees working in the public sector bank would prefer to continue the job as much as possible.

Working environment requires a mutual trust among managers and employees. Employees develop mistrust if firm set an incompatible target/manager withhold any important information passed on by the employees. It can be concluded at 1% level of significance that there is a statistical significant difference between the managers and employees perception towards no trust ($t = 4.665$, $p = 0.000$). Therefore managers working in the public sector banks were trustworthy and also it is proved that communications passed by employees were properly communicated to their management.

Uncertainty is nothing but doubt of employees and managers regarding their future obligation and commitment towards the achievement of organisational goal. It can be concluded at 5% level of significance that there is a statistical significant difference between the managers and employees perception towards uncertainty (t = 2.460, p = 0.014). Therefore managers were more confident about their future relationship with the employees at present employees was not in the position to predict their future relationship towards the manager working in public sector banks.

Employees do anticipate increased return for their contribution but unfortunately, if the expectation were not met it will erode the quality of work life. Since p value is above 5% level of significance it can be concluded that there is no statistical significant difference between the managers and employees perception towards erosion (t = 1.469, p = 0.143). Hence, in case erosion bank management did not reduce the employees and managers future benefits.

Employee fulfillment refers to the work obligated by the managers fulfilled by their employees. From the above it can be concluded at 1% level of significance that there is a statistical significant difference between the managers and employees towards employee fulfillment (t = 5.052, p = 0.000). Managers were more committed to fulfill their employee needs when compared to the employees.

Employer fulfillment refers to the work obligated by the employees fulfilled by their managers. It can be concluded at 1% level of significance that there is a statistical significant difference between the managers and employees towards employer fulfillment (t = 3.524, p = 0.000). Managers working in the public sector bank are fulfilling their obligations and live up the promises compared to their employees.

The findings of the Independent t test explain the perception of Employees and managers about ERM through psychological contract. Therefore it is statistically proved that there is a significant difference between perception of employees and managers working in public sector banks towards ERM.

4.3.3.2 *To analyze the effect of Psychological Empowerment Dimensions among Employees and Managers.*

Empowerment is considered as an effective self motivation tool through which employees and managers believe in themselves and co-operate to achieve their employment task easily and also it adds meaningfulness to their job. Psychological empowerment helps an individual to understand their attitude towards duty, responsibility, potentiality, and self-sufficiency at the work place. It might be more advantageous for managers to empower employees, through which they easily reach the organisational goal, thus encouraging the employee dependability helps in building a very good atmosphere of team work in turn results in greater employee performance. Meaning, competence, self determination and impact were considered as dimensions of the psychological empowerment.

Therefore to find out the perception differences about psychological empowerment among manager and employee and also to find the relationship between employees and manager working in the public sector bank through their psychological empowerment, Independent t test was performed. Independent t test helps to measure the significant differences between managers and employees perception towards psychological empowerment and also these differences help to analyze employee-manager relationship, capabilities and self determination to perform the work.

Hypotheses – 1.2

Null Hypotheses: There is no significant difference between work position and Psychological Empowerment Dimensions.

Table 4.3.3.2   T Test for Psychological Empowerment

Psychological empowerment Dimensions	Designation				T value	P value
	Manager		Employees			
	Mean	SD	Mean	SD		
Meaning	12.88	1.51	12.29	2.07	2.739	0.006**
Competence	12.79	1.43	12.68	1.74	0.622	0.535
Self Determination	11.93	1.69	11.46	2.09	2.134	0.034*

Psychological empowerment Dimensions	Designation				T value	P value
	Manager		Employees			
	Mean	SD	Mean	SD		
Impact	11.59	1.85	9.78	2.46	7.044	<0.000
Overall Psychological Empowerment	49.23	5.16	46.12	5.67	5.003	<0.000

** Denotes significant at 1% level. 2. * Denotes significant at 5% level

Meaning is used to measure the employees and managers value of their work objective. It helps to judge the relation to an individual's own ideals or standards. Meaning plays an important role by occupying a gap between work task and idea, ethics and behaviors required at work place. There is a significant difference between the managers and employees meaningfulness perceived through their job ($t = 2.739$, $p = 0.006$) at 1% level of significance. Therefore, when compared to employees, managers working in public sector banks were more empowered and view their job as more meaningful for their job.

Competence or self-efficacy is an individual's faith in his/her own talent to achieve organisational goal by using their maximum ability. Competence is considered to be the organisation faith towards its employees to achieve the expected performance. It can be concluded that even at 5% level of significance there is no statistical significant difference between the managers and employees perception towards competence ($t = 0.622$, $p = 0.535$).Therefore managers and employees maximum utilize the capabilities to achieve their employment tasks.

Where competence is a peak of behavior, self-determination is an individual's wisdom of containing a choice to begin and perform actions. Self-determination reflects on employee's independence mainly during their commencement and continuation towards making decisions about work methods, pace and effort. It can be concluded at 5% level of significance that there is a significant difference between the managers and employees towards the perception of their self-determination ($t = 2.134$, $p = 0.034$). Therefore managers working in the public sector banks are having more choice to initiate and also to regulate his/her own actions.

Impact is used to measure the amount to which an individual in the organisation are able to influence the managerially planned working results. Impact is observed as a communication of learned exposure. Further, Impact is different from locus of control; whereas impact is influenced by the work context; internal locus of control is a global personality characteristic that endures across situations. It can be concluded at 1% level of significance that there is a statistical significant difference between the managers and employees perception towards degree of impact towards their job (t = 7.044, p = <0.000). Therefore manager's impact is higher than that of their employees.

The findings of the Independent t test explain the perception differences between employees and managers about ERM through psychological empowerment. Except in case of competence all other dimensions in psychological empowerment have significance difference. On the whole i.e., overall psychological empowerment statistically proved that there is a significant difference between perception of employees and managers working in public sector banks towards ERM.

4.3.3.3   *To examine the difference between employees and managers towards their Involvement at Work.*

Higher involvement is presumed to enhance motivation in two different ways. First, it is considered to be intrinsically valued, so that employees are more likely to emotionally invest in jobs that provide rewards of self-determination. Second, opportunities for decision making process provide satisfying working conditions and match employee's expectations. Involvement helps every individual in the organisation to take part actively in the decision regarding their work. It further helps to understand one's own power i.e., capabilities to perform their task easily even in critical situations. Involvement makes the employees to engage in the work and seeks information. Further it results them to innovate new techniques/ideas to attain the organisational goal. Therefore it increases job satisfaction and also increases the workforce retention rates. Reward, knowledge, information and power were considered as the dimensions of employee involvement.

Independent t test facilitates to determine the significant differences between managers and employees perception towards their Involvement and also these differences help to analyze employee-manager relationship, their satisfaction towards information, reward, knowledge and power to perform their work efficiently.

Hypotheses – 1.3

Null Hypotheses: There is no significant difference between work position and Employee Involvement Dimensions.

Table 4.3.3.3   T Test for Employee Involvement

Dimensions of Employee Involvement	Designation				t value	P value
	Manager		Employee			
	Mean	SD	Mean	SD		
Information	15.63	2.46	14.82	2.36	2.977	.003**
Reward	11.10	2.22	10.31	2.35	3.060	.002**
Knowledge	11.29	2.04	10.70	2.10	2.517	.012*
Power	10.69	2.16	9.70	2.69	3.440	.001**
Overall Involvement	48.70	7.77	45.67	8.32	3.302	.001**

** Denotes significant at 1% level. 2. * Denotes significant at 5% level

Information is considered as rights and obligation of every individual in an organisation. This information helps them to share their knowledge through which they attain their organisational task easily. Clear communication leads to half work done, therefore, managers working in the public sector bank need to share and discuss the important information so as to increase their employee's involvement. There is a significant difference between the managers and employees towards information received to perform their job efficiently ($t = 2.977$, $p = 0.003$). Therefore when compared to employees managers working in public sector banks get more information to perform their duty through which they actively get involved in their work.

Reward is considered as an important element that affects the outcome of employee involvement, which is the feedback for employees to acquire power, information, and knowledge. There is a significant difference between the managers and employees towards reward received from their work ($t = 3.060$, $p = 0.002$) at 1% level of significance. Therefore, when compared to employees, managers working in public sector banks receive more rewards for the active participation.

Knowledge facilitates an individual in the organisation to know and contribute the appropriate techniques, potentiality and professional skills of employees to attain their organisational goal. There is a significant difference between the managers and employees knowledge about the technique used to perform their duty effectively as well as efficiently (t = 2.517, p = 0.012) at 5% level of significance. Managers were more aware of appropriate technique to be used in their job rather compared to employees.

Power is believed as the most influencing factor in decision making process. Manager in the branch by giving adequate authorities to other officers and employees working with him increase the branch potentiality. There is a significant difference between the managers and employees degree of power to perform their job efficiently (t = 3.440, p = 0.001) at 1% level of significance. Manager power in decision making is higher than that of their employees.

The findings of the Independent t test explain the perception of employees and managers about ERM through employee involvement. It is statistically proved that there is a significant difference between perception of employees and managers working in public sector banks towards ERM.

4.3.3.4   *To analyze the difference between Employees and Managers Cultural Intelligence*

In today's competitive world it is the duty of every individual in the organisation to be prepared to serve their customers. India is culturally diversified nation where every individual in the organisation should be aware of other cultural customs and languages. Further they must be ready to adopt different culture so as to receive support from employees of other culture. This helps to build an efficient and effective team that leads to good customer service and support. For this purpose Meta cognitive, cognitive, motivational and behavioral were considered as the dimensions of cultural intelligence.

Thus, to find the perception differences regarding cultural intelligence among managers and employees working in the public sector bank and also to find the relationship between them through their cultural knowledge, Independent t test was performed. Independent t test helps to measure the significant differences between managers and employees perception towards cultural intelligence and also these differences analyze the employee-manager relationship and their cultural knowledge in order to the work place.

Hypotheses – 1.4

Null Hypotheses: There is no significant difference between work position and Cultural Intelligence Dimensions.

Table 4.3.3.4 T Test for Cultural Intelligence.

Dimensions of Cultural intelligence	Designation				T value	P value
	Manager		Employee			
	Mean	SD	Mean	SD		
Meta cognitive	15.59	2.27	15.22	2.45	1.376	0.170
Cognitive	20.59	4.34	19.56	4.35	2.113	0.035*
Motivational	18.50	2.91	17.47	3.27	2.873	0.004**
Behavioral	18.46	2.88	18.58	3.36	0.318	0.751
Overall Cultural Intelligence	73.50	11.32	69.48	12.55	2.923	0.004**

** Denotes significant at 1% level. 2. * Denotes significant at 5% level

Meta cognitive means how an individual makes good judgment about other culture. This in turn replicates the method through which an individual obtain knowledge about other culture. It can be concluded even at 5% level of significance that there is no statistical significant difference between the managers and employees towards meta cognitive (t = 1.376, p = 0.170). It can be further concluded that there is no significant difference between employees and managers experience towards the other culture. Therefore managers and employees have to take necessary steps to acquire and understand the other culture to the maximum limit.

Cognitive refers to how employees understand differences and similarities between the cultures. This cultural knowledge helps them to understand other culture systems. There is a statistical significant difference between the managers and employees towards knowledge about the other culture (t = 2.113, p = 0.035) at 5% level of significance. When compared to employees, managers working in public sector banks have comparatively high cultural knowledge especially about the legal system, religious beliefs which in-turn helps the manager to establish bond with employees.

Motivation in cultural intelligence is explained as an employee's interest in practicing and interacting with other culture employees. This in turn help them to learn about other culture further will motivate employee functioning in cross-cultural situation. There is a statistical significant difference between the managers and employees motivation towards experiencing other culture (t = 2.873, p = 0.004) at 1% level of significance. Hence managers get more opportunities to interact with persons from other culture than that of employees. This helps the managers to understand their cross cultural employee's value.

Behavior in the cultural intelligence enlightens an employee's skill to adopt verbal and non verbal behavior towards other culture. There is no statistical significant difference between the managers and employees towards verbal and non-behavioral response (t = 0.318, p = 0.751). Therefore it can be concluded that managers and employees behavioral responses that are appropriate in various situations and have the capability to modify based on interaction with other culture individual.

The findings of Independent t test explain the perception of employees and managers about ERM through Cultural intelligence. Therefore it is statistically proved that there is a significant difference between perception of employees and managers working in public sector banks towards ERM.

4.3.3.5   *To analyze the perception difference between Employees and Managers towards Psychological Ownership, Organisational Support and In Role Performance.*

Psychological ownership is the inner feeling of possession of every individual in the organisation. It gives them a pride and will erase the ill-feeling of having worked for others. In turn it keeps them aware and will educate about the organisational products and clients. This self realization helps an individual to be empowered and achieve their organisational task easily.

Perceived Organisational Support (POS) refers to employees' perception concerning the extent to which the organisation values their contribution and cares about their well being. POS has been found to have important consequences mainly in employee's performance and well-being. In short, organisational support means support received by an individual in the organisation from their supervisors in order to complete the task.

Inrole performance means level of achievement made by an individual in the organisation from assigned duties. On the basis of achievement, rewards and recognition should be given to employees further it encourage employees to take active participation in the management. Feedback system motivates employees for their better performance.

In order to analyze the perception differences about other dimensions of ERM such as perceived organisational support, psychological ownership and inrole performance among manager and employee and also to understand the relationship between employees and manager working in the public sector bank through their POS, PO and IRP, Independent t test was carried out. Independent t test facilitates to determine the significant differences between managers and employees perception towards their POS, PO and IRP. Further these differences help to analyze employee-manager relationship perform their work efficiently.

Hypotheses – 1.5

Null Hypotheses: There is no significant difference between work position Psychological Ownership, Organisational Support and In Role Performance.

Table 4.3.3.5   T Test for Psychological Ownership, Organisational Support and in Role Performance.

Dimensions of ERM	Designation				T value	P value
	Manager		Employee			
	Mean	SD	Mean	SD		
Psychological ownership	30.16	4.75	27.66	4.87	4.592	<0.000
Organisational support	29.31	4.57	27.49	5.05	3.304	0.001**
In role performance	27.20	3.28	25.73	3.74	3.629	<0.000

** Denotes significant at 1% level.

Psychological ownership is a state of emotional feeling by every individual in the organisation. This feeling make employees and managers working in the public sector bank to attain empathy towards their organisation. There is a statistical significant difference between the managers and employees perception towards level of psychological ownership perceived from their work and from the employers (t = 4.592, p = 0.000) at 1% level of significance. Level of ownership feeling perceived by the managers is higher than that of his/her employees.

Organisational support means support received by employees from their employer to perform the organisational duties. It is considered to be a most important tool in every organisation to motivate and engage the employees towards organisational goal. It further helps employees to add meaningfulness to their job. There is a statistical significant difference between the managers and employees perception towards their organisational support (t = 3.304, p = 0.001) at 1% level of significance. Hence organisational support received by the managers to perform their work is greater than what his/her employees received.

Employees use awards and achievement to turn the spot light on them. There is a statistical significant difference between the managers and employees towards in role performance (t = 3.629, p = <0.000) at 1% level of significance. Managers performance is comparatively high than his/her employees.

The findings of the Independent t test explain the perception of employees and managers about ERM through psychological ownership, organisational support and in role performance. Therefore it is statistically proved that there is a significant difference between perception of employees and managers working in public sector banks towards ERM.

4.3.4 TO IDENTIFY THE DIFFERENCES BETWEEN EMPLOY-EES AND MANAGERS WITH REGARDS TO PSYCHOLOG-ICAL WELL-BEING, ORGANISATIONAL COMMITMENT AND ORGANISATIONAL CITIZENSHIP BEHAVIOR.

Work place is to be kept most ideal for the employees and welfare activities are to be improved. Employer should create a family like atmosphere in the office so that the employees can take part in all the developmental activities and do not complain much. Pledging the ego by both will improve the working atmosphere. Development of real human relations and discipline among employees at all levels will in turn make employees to feel that their bank really has concern for their well being.

Hypotheses – 2

Null Hypotheses: There is no significant difference between work position PW, OC, and OCB.

Table 4.3.4 T Test for Individual Well-Being and Work Place Behavior

Dependent variable	Designation				T value	P value
	Manager		Employees			
	Mean	SD	Mean	SD		
Psychological wellbeing	215.53	24.61	208.24	23.94	2.680	0.008**
Commitment	64.61	7.99	62.93	7.87	1.881	0.061
Organisational citizenship behavior	94.13	14.10	91.31	13.84	1.799	0.073

** Denotes significant at 1% level.

Since P value is less than 0.01 in case of psychological well-being, the null hypothesis is rejected at 1% level of significance. Hence it is concluded that there is significant difference between employees and managers working in the public sector bank towards the psychological well-being perceived from their job. But this was not the situation with reference to commitment and citizenship behavior. Even at 5% both are insignificant. It shows that there is no significance difference between employees and managers level of commitment and their work place behavior.

4.3.4.1   *To analyze the employees and managers difference while perceiving their wellbeing from their work.*

The art of knowing and knowing is defined as psychological well being. Employers are constantly in the know and transfer that knowledge to subordinates and involve people effectively. Having the basics placed strategically only drives employees to align themselves with the organisational goals and keep them completely engaged and motivated. Workplace well being is largely connected to health and wellness. It influences three psychological dimensions that are workplace, workforce and the work people do. Based on reviews Work Involvement, Intrinsic Job Motivation, High Order Need, Perceived Intrinsic Job Characteristic, Life Satisfaction, Job Satisfaction, Happiness and Self Anxiety were considered as the dimensions of psychological well-being.

In order to analyze the perception differences about psychological well-being among manager and employee and also to understand the relationship between employees and manager working in the public sector bank through their Well-being, Independent t test was carried out. Independent t test determine the significant differences between managers and employees perception towards their involvement and also these differences help to analyze employee-manager relationship, their satisfaction towards work environment, life and happiness to perform their work efficiently.

Hypotheses – 2.1

Null Hypotheses: There is no significant difference between work position and Psychological Wellbeing Dimensions.

Table 4.3.4.1 T Test For Dimensions of Psychological Well-Being.

Psychological well-being Dimensions	Designation				T value	P value
	Manager		Employees			
	Mean	SD	Mean	SD		
Job Satisfaction	54.41	6.47	51.87	7.65	3.089	.002**
Work Involvement	15.17	2.15	14.96	2.33	0.835	0.404
Intrinsic Job Motivation	24.79	2.61	24.66	2.94	0.398	0.691
High Order Need	24.16	2.55	22.92	3.39	3.482	.001**
Perceived Intrinsic Job Characteristic	31.31	3.30	29.93	4.60	2.902	.004**
Life Satisfaction	37.78	4.00	37.58	5.37	0.361	0.718
Happiness	3.92	.68	3.81	.92	1.141	0.255
Self Anxiety	24.25	2.41	24.03	2.94	0.715	0.475
Overall Psychological wellbeing	215.53	24.61	208.24	23.94	2.680	.008**

** Denotes significant at 1% level.

Job satisfaction is the degree to which a person reports satisfaction with intrinsic and extrinsic features of the job. Total job satisfaction is the sum of all separate items, and overall job satisfaction is reported satisfaction with the job as a whole. There is a significant difference between the managers and employees perception towards job satisfaction (t = 3.089, p = 0.002) at 1% level of significance. Level of satisfaction perceived from the job by the managers is higher than that of their employee's satisfaction level.

Work involvement is viewed as the degree to which a person wants to be engaged in work. There is no statistical significant difference between the managers and employees towards work involvement (t = 0.835, p = 0.404). Therefore managers and employees level of engagement towards their organisational task is quite same.

Intrinsic job motivation is viewed as the degree to which a person wants to work well in his or her job in order to achieve intrinsic satisfaction. There is no statistical significant difference between the managers and employees group's mean towards intrinsic job motivation perceived from their job (t = 0.398, p = 0.691). Therefore managers and employees level of motivation to attain their organisational task is quite same.

Higher order need strength is taken to be the importance which a person attaches to the attainment of higher order needs. There is a statistical significant difference between the managers and employees perception towards their high order need (t = 3.482, p = 0.001) at 1% level of significance. High order need of managers is higher than that of their employees.

Perceived intrinsic job characteristics are the person's reports about the degree to which features are present in his or her job which might give rise to intrinsic satisfaction. There is a statistical significant difference between the managers and employees towards perceived intrinsic job characteristics (t = 2.902, p = 0.004) at 1% level of significance. Hence managers have greater amount of intrinsic satisfaction from his/her job rather than his/her employees.

Life satisfaction is the degree to which a person reports satisfaction with salient features of his life and life-space. Total life satisfaction is the sum of all separate items, and overall life satisfaction is reported satisfaction with one's life as a whole. It can be concluded even at 5% level of significance that there is no statistical significant difference between the managers and employees life satisfaction perceived from their personal life (t = 0.361, p = 0.718). Therefore managers and employees life satisfaction is quite same.

Happiness is the degree to which a person reports that he or she is currently happy. It can be concluded even at 5% level of significance that there is no statistical significant difference between the managers and employees managers level of happiness perceived from their personal life (t = 1.141, p = 0.255). Therefore managers and employees level of happiness perceived from their personal life is quite same.

Self-rated anxiety is the degree to which a person reports anxiety about salient features of his or her life and life-space summed across items, and overall self-rated anxiety is reported anxiety in general. It can be concluded even at 5% level of significance that there is no statistical significant difference between the managers and employees self anxiety derived from their personal life (t = 0.715, p = 0.475). Therefore managers and employees level of anxiety is same.

The findings of the Independent t test explain the perception of Employees and managers about psychological well-being. Therefore it is statistically proved that there is a significant difference between perception of employees and managers working in public sector banks towards psychological well-being.

4.3.4.2 *To find out the employees and managers difference towards commitment in their work.*

An employee who is completely involved in his work is called as an engaged employee and the engaged employees aim to achieve the organisational objective. An engaged team only furthers the interest of the organisation in a positive manner. This results in optimization of workforce that helps to retain talent for time to come even when opportunities to move on exist. Based on the review Affective, Continuance and Normative commitment were considered as dimensions of Organisational Commitment.

Independent t test facilitates to determine the significant differences between managers and employees perception towards their commitment and also these differences help to analyze employee-manager relationship in order to perform their work efficiently.

Hypotheses – 2.2

Null Hypotheses: There is no significant difference between work position and Organisational Commitment Dimensions.

Table 4.3.4.2   T Test For Dimensions of Organisational Commitment.

Organisational Commitment Dimensions	Designation				T value	P value
	Manager		Employees			
	Mean	SD	Mean	SD		
Affective commitment	22.64	3.93	21.70	3.95	2.114	.035*
Continuance Commitment	20.72	3.66	20.35	3.44	.935	.350

Organisational Commitment Dimensions	Designation				T value	P value
	Manager		Employees			
	Mean	SD	Mean	SD		
Normative commitment	21.24	0.21	20.88	3.63	.931	.352
Overall Commitment	64.61	7.99	62.93	7.87	1.881	.061

* Denotes significant at 5% level

In order to compete effectively, employers need to go above and beyond satisfaction. Employers must do their best to inspire and keep their employees glued to apply their full potential and capabilities at work. There is a statistical significant difference between the managers and employees perception towards the affective commitment (t = 2.114, p = 0.035) at 5% level of significance. Managers have greater amount of emotional attachment than that his/her employees towards organisation.

Continuance commitment measures the intention of employees and managers working in the public sector bank to continue their job till the retirement. It can be concluded even at 5% level of significance that there is no statistical significant difference between the managers and employees perception towards continuance commitment (t = 0.935, p = 0.350). Therefore managers and employees both are willing to continue their job in the same bank.

The contemporary or modern organisations expect their employees to be full of enthusiasm and show initiative at work, they want them to take responsibility for their own development, strive for high excellence and performance, be full of rigor and dedicated to what they do. It can be concluded even at 5% level of significance that there is no statistical significant difference between the managers and employees perception towards normative commitment (t = 0.931, p = 0.352). Therefore managers and employees working in the public sector bank believe that they are needed by the organisation.

The findings of the Independent t test explain the perception of employees and managers towards their Organisational commitment. Therefore it is statistically proved that there is no significant difference between employees and managers working in public sector banks towards their commitment.

4.3.4.3 *To find out the employees and managers difference towards their citizenship behavior in the bank.*

Another strong element of organisational citizenship behavior is personal initiative. A worker with good OCB will often be able to take charge of a situation with little direction. This kind of employee typically has an innate understanding of what needs to be done in order to promote organisational goals. Employees who practice OCB tend to be strong ambassadors for the company brand as well. For research purpose Altruism, Conscientiousness, Courtesy, Civic Virtue and Sportsmanship are considered as dimensions of OCB.

Therefore to analyze the perception differences regarding OCB among manager and employee and also to understand the relationship between employees and manager working in the public sector bank through their citizenship behavior, Independent t test is carried out. Independent t test facilitates to determine the significant differences between managers and employees perception towards their OCB and also these differences help to analyze employee-manager relationship in order to perform their work efficiently.

Hypotheses – 2.1

Null Hypotheses: There is no significant difference between work position and Organisational Citizenship Behavior Dimensions.

Table 4.3.4.3 T Test for Dimensions of Organisational Citizenship Behavior.

Organisational Citizenship Behavior Dimensions	Designation				T value	P value
	Manager		Employees			
	Mean	SD	Mean	SD		
Altruism	20.30	2.72	19.90	2.34	1.409	0.160
Conscientiousness	20.78	1.94	20.01	2.28	3.157	0.002**
Courtesy	20.51	1.85	19.98	2.15	2.282	0.023*
Civic Virtue	19.78	2.08	18.58	2.25	4.844	<0.000

Organisational Citizenship Behavior Dimensions	Designation				T value	P value
	Manager		Employees			
	Mean	SD	Mean	SD		
Sportsmanship	18.10	3.17	17.89	3.14	.599	0.550
Organisational citizenship behavior	94.13	14.10	91.31	13.84	1.799	0.073

** Denotes significant at 1% level. 2. * Denotes significant at 5% level

Altruism is a voluntary behavior where an employee provides assistance to an individual with a particular problem to complete his or her task under unusual circumstances. In case of Altruism, it can be concluded that there is no statistically significant difference between the managers and employees group mean towards altruism (t = 1.409, p = 0.160). It can also be said that even at 5% level of significance there is no significant difference between employees and managers altruism at their work place. Therefore managers and employees helping other individual in the organisation in their work place are quite similar.

Conscientiousness is used to indicate that a particular individual is organised, accountable and hardworking. There is a statistically significant difference between the managers and employees group mean towards Conscientiousness (t = 3.157, p = 0.002) at 1% level of significance. Therefore managers and employees level of dedication to achieve their organisational task is quite not the same. It can also be concluded that managers are considered to be more dedicated and hard working than his/her employees.

Courtesy includes behaviors, which focus on the prevention of problems and taking the necessary step so as to lessen the effects of the problem in the future. In other words, courtesy means a member encourages other workers when they are demoralized and feel discouraged about their professional development. There is a statistically significant difference between the managers and employees group mean towards Courtesy (t = 2.282, p = 0.023) at 5% level of significance. Therefore managers and employees perception of inter group conflict differ. Hence it can also be said that manager's behavior focuses on the prevention of problems and taking essential steps to minimize the effects of the problem in the future than his/her employees.

Civic virtue refers to the responsibility of the subordinates to participate in the life of the firm such as attending meetings which are not required by the firm and keeping up with the changes in the organisation. There is a statistically significant difference between the managers and employees group mean towards civic virtue (t = 4.844, p = <0.000) at 1% level of significance. It can be further concluded at 1% level of significance that there is a significant difference between employees and managers perception towards their civic virtue. It is proved that bank managers allow their employee to participate in the meetings and administrative functions of the organisation.

Sportsmanship is the behavior of warmly tolerating the irritations that are unavoidable part of nearly every organisational setting. There is no statistically significant difference between the managers and employees group mean towards Sportsmanship (t = 0.599, p = 0.550) even at 5% level of significance. Therefore managers and employees level of tolerance is quite same.

In the recent times it is seen that an individual's behavior has brought an organisation down and an individual's good citizenship behavior has pushed the organisation to greater limits. An employer or employee practicing OCB tends to be more committed to the job than the ones who are not.

The findings of the Independent t test explain the perception of Employees and managers about Organisational citizenship behavior. Therefore it is statistically proved that there is no significant difference between employees and managers working in public sector banks towards organisational citizenship behavior.

4.3.5 TO EVALUATE MANAGERS AND EMPLOYEES PERCEP-TION TOWARDS ERM DIMENSIONS AND PSYCHOLOG-ICAL WELL-BEING, ORGANISATIONAL COMMITMENT AND ORGANISATIONAL CITIZENSHIP BEHAVIOR BASED ON THEIR PERSONAL CHARACTERISTICS.

In order to know the perception of ERM between employees and managers dimensions of ERM was compared with the personal factors so as to understand whether their personal characteristics influence their perception. Psychological contract, psychological empowerment, psychological ownership, cultural intelligence, organisational support, employee involvement, psychological well being, organisational commitment, and organisational citizenship behavior and in role performance were assumed as the dimensions of ERM. Demographic characters such as age, gender, marital status, income and work experience were considered as personal characteristics.

Independent t test was used where there are only two groups where as ANOVA was performed where there are more than two groups.

Hypotheses – 3

There is no significant difference between income group and ERM Dimensions and PW, OC, OCB for Employees and Managers.

In case of Psychological contract (PC), it can be concluded that even at 5% level of significance there is no significant difference between the income of employees ($f = 0.907$, $p = 0.437$) and managers ($f = 0.132$, $p = 0.877$) towards psychological contract and manager.

In case of Psychological empowerment (PE), it can be concluded that even at 5% level of significance there is no statistical significant difference between the income of employees ($f = 1.152$, $p = 0.329$) and managers ($f = 0.500$, $p = 0.608$) towards psychological empowerment.

In case of Employee involvement (EI), it can be concluded that even at 5% level of significance there is no significant difference between the income of employees ($f = 2.156$, $p = 0.094$) and managers ($f = 0.746$, $p = 0.477$) towards involvement.

In case of Cultural Intelligence (CI), it can be concluded that even at 5% level of significance there is no significant difference between the income of employees ($f = 2.001$, $p = 0.114$) and managers ($f = 0.783$, $p = 0.460$) towards involvement.

In case of Psychological ownership (PO), it can be concluded that even at 5% level of significance there is no significant difference between the income of employees ($f = 0.595$, $p = 0.619$) and managers ($f = 0.450$, $p = 0.639$) towards psychological ownership.

In case of Organisational support (OS), it can be concluded that even at 5% level of significance there is a significant difference between the income of employees ($f = 3.638$, $p = 0.013$) and there is no statistical significant difference between the income of managers ($f = 0.870$, $p = 0.422$) towards organisational support.

Table 4.3.5.1 Anova for Income, ERM Dimensions, PW, OC and OCB.

IV	Employees						Managers				
	Annual Salary in Lakhs				F value	P value	Annual Salary in Lakhs			F value	P value
	Up to 3	3 – 5	5 - 7	Above 7			3 – 5	5 - 7	Above 7		
PC	138.43 (18.23)	141.02 (18.60)	137.55 (17.81)	146.57 (22.06)	.909	.437	150.25 (10.64)	152.25 (14.10)	152.07 (14.41)	.132	.877
PE	46.71 (5.78)	46.15 (5.69)	45.28 (5.45)	48.14 (6.52)	1.152	.329	50.44 (5.61)	49.05 (5.13)	49.04 (5.11)	.500	.608
EI	46.33 (8.26)	46.04 (8.51)	44.07 (8.01)	51.00 (7.79)	2.156	.094	47.00 (9.76)	49.66 (6.60)	48.44 (8.04)	.746	.477
CI	69.77 (13.10)	70.71 (12.26)	67.13 (12.06)	76.86 (12.02)	2.001	.114	76.75 (9.62)	72.73 (10.96)	73.16 (12.06)	.783	.460
PO	27.84 (5.17)	27.09 (4.92)	28.04 (4.39)	28.14 (6.07)	.595	.619	29.25 (3.55)	30.05 (4.66)	30.51 (5.15)	.450	.639
OS	28.06 (5.39)	28.13 (5.08)	25.96 (4.32)	29.57 (5.13)	3.638	.013*	27.94 (3.75)	29.66 (4.30)	29.44 (4.97)	.870	.422

Table 4.3.5.1   *(Contd.)*

IV	Employees						Managers				
	Annual Salary in Lakhs				F value	P value	Annual Salary in Lakhs			F value	P value
	Up to 3	3 – 5	5 - 7	Above 7			3 – 5	5 - 7	Above 7		
IRP	25.80 (3.40)	25.79 (4.27)	25.34 (3.35)	28.29 (4.31)	1.388	.247	26.88 (3.83)	27.20 (3.51)	27.29 (2.95)	.098	.906
PW	206.95 (24.89)	208.01 (26.20)	209.24 (18.88)	215.14 (35.69)	.317	.813	218.13 (18.53)	214.11 (28.63)	215.91 (22.95)	.166	.847
OC	62.72 (7.53)	63.33 (8.15)	62.66 (8.05)	63.57 (8.10)	.137	.938	66.38 (6.87)	64.23 (8.04)	64.40 (8.31)	.456	.635
OCB	92.13 (13.15)	91.86 (14.34)	89.95 (13.83)	89.71 (17.45)	.415	.742	98.50 (10.78)	92.14 (15.67)	94.45 (13.51)	1.229	.297

* Denotes significant at 5% level

In case of In role performance (IRP), it can be concluded that even at 5% level of significance there is no significant difference between the income of employees (f = 1.388, p = 0.247)and managers (f = 0.098, p = 0.906) towards in role performance.

In case of Psychological well-being (PW), it can be concluded that even at 5% level of significance there is no significant difference between the income of employees (f = 0.317, p = 0.813)and managers (f = 0.166, p = 0.847) towards the well-being perceived from both work and from personal.

In case of Organisational commitment (OC), it can be concluded that even at 5% level of significance there is no significant difference between the income of employees (f = 0.137, p = 0.938) and managers (f = 0.456, p = 0.635) towards the level of commitment to complete their organisational task.

In case of Organisational citizenship behavior (OCB), it can be concluded that even at 5% level of significance there is no significant difference between the income of employees (f = 0.415, p = 0.742) and managers (f = 1.229, p = 0.297) towards their work place behavior.

Results of ANOVA for Income Categories and ERM Dimensions, PW, OC and OCB

As far as the mean scores of psychological contract, psychological empowerment, employee involvement, cultural intelligence, psychological ownership, perceived organisational support and in role performance are concerned the test result indicates that no significant difference exists between ERM dimensions, individual well-being dimensions, work place behavior and various income categories.

This may be due to that the employees and managers working in the public sector banks have same perception towards certain ERM dimensions, individual well-being dimensions and work place behavior. But in case of employees organisational support was influenced by the income group especially employees earning between 5-7lakhs whose mean score is low when compared to other income levels; this may be because employees earning between 5-7lakhs expects more support from their managers. The result indicates that there is no significant relationship between Income group and individual well-being and their work place behavior.

Hypotheses – 4

There is no significant difference between age group and ERM Dimensions and PW, OC, OCB for Employees and Managers.

Table 4.3.5.2   Anova for Age, ERM Dimensions, PW, OC and OCB.

IV & DV	Employees						Managers					
	Age Group in years				F value	P value	Age Group in years				F value	P value
	Below 30	31-40	41-50	Above 50			Below 30	31-40	41-50	Above 50		
PC	140.26 (18.48)	139.05 (20.82)	137.15 (17.87)	139.86 (17.45)	.350	.789	141.60 (8.08)	151.13 (13.57)	151.05 (12.23)	152.95 (14.33)	1.127	.341
PE	46.54 (6.01)	46.05 (6.27)	46.65 (5.19)	45.36 (5.37)	.774	.509	53.00 (4.36)	50.87 (6.13)	49.30 (4.82)	48.64 (5.01)	1.753	.160
EI	46.64 (8.54)	45.22 (8.85)	45.29 (8.76)	45.17 (7.56)	.528	.664	41.20 (8.98)	51.60 (6.40)	50.40 (6.60)	48.17 (7.95)	2.810	.043
CI	70.20 (13.76)	70.11 (13.13)	70.71 (12.53)	67.59 (10.92)	.883	.451	78.60 (12.16)	75.80 (10.32)	72.50 (12.07)	72.96 (11.34)	.647	.586

Table 4.3.5.2 *(Contd.)*

IV & DV	Employees						Managers					
	Age Group in years				F value	P value	Age Group in years				F value	P value
	Below 30	31-40	41-50	Above 50			Below 30	31-40	41-50	Above 50		
PO	27.13 (5.36)	26.89 (5.33)	28.75 (4.24)	27.79 (4.46)	1.57	.197	29.80 (3.27)	29.93 (5.23)	30.10 (4.71)	30.24 (4.83)	.028	.994
OS	27.39 (6.02)	28.38 (4.02)	27.65 (5.00)	27.05 (4.42)	.606	.612	28.20 (4.38)	29.87 (3.23)	29.60 (4.82)	29.20 (4.79)	.210	.889
IRP	25.54 (3.80)	25.22 (4.31)	26.27 (3.59)	25.78 (3.50)	.693	.557	23.20 (2.95)	28.80 (4.02)	26.85 (2.32)	27.24 (3.16)	4.056	.009**
PW	208.38 (25.19)	204.78 (28.64)	210.29 (23.50)	208.28 (20.57)	.390	.761	224.60 (23.73)	207.60 (31.48)	219.95 (27.59)	215.33 (22.27)	.961	.414
OC	61.88 (8.19)	62.19 (7.66)	64.62 (8.74)	63.18 (6.86)	1.465	.225	65.20 (4.32)	64.87 (9.42)	64.00 (7.39)	64.68 (8.15)	.054	.984
OCB	92.25 (14.46)	89.08 (12.15)	94.80 (15.34)	88.94 (12.38)	2.414	.067	99.20 (13.81)	92.87 (19.54)	91.05 (11.84)	94.87 (13.51)	.636	.593

In case of Psychological contract (PC), it can be concluded that even at 5% level of significance there is no significant difference between the age group of employees (f = 0.350, p = 0.789) and managers (f = 0.1127, p = 0.341) towards their psychological contract.

In case of Psychological empowerment (PE), it can be concluded that even at 5% level of significance there is no significant difference between the age group of employees (f = 0.774, p = 0.509) and managers (f = 1.753, p = 0.160) towards their psychological empowerment.

In case of Employee involvement (EI), it can be concluded that even at 5% level of significance there is no significant difference between the age group of employees (f = 0.528, p = 0.664) and there is a significant difference between the age group of managers (f = 2.810, p = 0.043) towards the level of involvement at their work.

In case of Cultural Intelligence (CI), it can be concluded that even at 5% level of significance there is no significant difference between the age group of employees (f = 0.883, p = 0.451) and managers (f = 0.647, p = 0.586) towards the level of cultural knowledge.

In case of Psychological ownership (PO), it can be concluded that even at 5% level of significance there is no significant difference between the age group of employees (f = 1.571, p = 0.197) and managers (f = 0.028, p = 0.994) towards the psychological ownership feeling about their banks.

In case of Organisational support (OS), it can be concluded that even at 5% level of significance there is no significant difference between the age group of employees (f = 0.606, p = 0.612) and managers (f = 0.210, p = 0.899) towards the organisational support received from their banks.

In case of In role performance (IRP), it can be concluded that even at 5% level of significance there is no significant difference between the age group of employees (f = 0.693, p = 0.557) and at 1% level of significance there is a significant difference between the age group of managers (f = 4.056, p = 0.009) towards their level of performance at work.

In case of Psychological well-being (PW), it can be concluded that even at 5% level of significance there is no significant difference between the age group of employees ($f = 0.390$, $p = 0.761$) and managers ($f = 0.961$, $p = 0.414$) towards the well-being perceived from both work and from personal.

In case of Organisational commitment (OC), it can be concluded that even at 5% level of significance there is no significant difference between the age group of employees ($f = 1.465$, $p = 0.225$) and managers ($f = 0.054$, $p = 0.984$) towards the level of commitment to complete their organisational task.

In case of Organisational citizenship behavior (OCB), it can be concluded that even at 5% level of significance there is no significant difference between the age group of employees ($f = 2.414$, $p = 0.067$) and managers ($f = 0.636$, $p = 0.593$) towards the behavior at their work place.

Results of ANOVA for Age Group, ERM Dimensions PW, OC and OCB

The test result of ANOVA indicates that there is no significant difference between age group of employees and managers towards certain ERM dimensions. The mean differences of employees and managers working in the public sector banks explain that involvement and performance were influenced by their age group. This may be because newly promoted managers have higher career expectation.

The findings of the one way ANOVA explain the perception of employees and managers about the psychological well-being, level of commitment and citizenship behavior at their work place. The mean score of the older age and the younger age group is quite similar with regards to PW, OC and OCB. This may be because younger group employees expectations might be achieved at work place.

This finding was supported by Waldman and Avolio (1986) in which they found there is a positive relationship between age group and performance. Further, this result was supported by Cleveland and Shore (1992) in which they concluded that age continues to be an important predictor for work variables.

Hypotheses–5

There is no significant difference between level of education and ERM Dimensions and PW, OC, OCB for Employees and Managers.

Table 4.3.5.3 Anova for Education, ERM Dimensions, PW, OC and OCB.

IV	Employees					Manager				
	Educational Qualification			F value	P value	Educational Qualification			F value	P value
	UG	PG	Others			UG	PG	Others		
PC	139.46 (17.58)	138.85 (18.99)	139.83 (21.76)	.355	.701	153.03 (14.46)	149.54 (12.92)	153.71 (10.16)	.868	.422
PE	46.03 (5.76)	46.44 (5.78)	45.28 (4.56)	.069	.933	49.28 (5.39)	49.05 (5.14)	49.86 (3.08)	.076	.927
EI	45.84 (8.14)	45.45 (8.65)	45.39 (8.49)	.138	.871	49.38 (7.84)	47.36 (7.87)	49.57 (6.40)	.884	.416
CI	69.14 (11.35)	70.03 (13.97)	69.56 (14.98)	.107	.898	73.19 (11.40)	73.62 (11.71)	75.86 (9.41)	.177	.838
PO	27.76 (4.55)	27.56 (5.54)	27.28 (3.91)	.838	.434	30.87 (4.55)	29.05 (5.07)	29.29 (4.19)	1.980	.143

Table 4.3.5.3 (*Contd.*)

IV	Employees					Manager				
	Educational Qualification			F value	P value	Educational Qualification			F value	P value
	UG	PG	Others			UG	PG	Others		
OS	27.69 (4.68)	27.45 (5.54)	26.06 (5.44)	.274	.760	29.77 (4.76)	28.41 (4.38)	29.86 (3.24)	1.158	.318
IRP	25.81 (3.70)	25.73 (3.81)	25.11 (3.86)	.954	.387	27.90 (3.22)	26.10 (3.35)	26.43 (1.27)	4.167	.018*
PW	209.22 (22.55)	205.68 (26.68)	212.83 (20.37)	1.030	.359	218.81 (22.39)	210.05 (26.85)	213.71 (30.67)	1.616	.203
OC	63.43 (7.60)	61.97 (8.39)	63.67 (7.37)	1.834	.162	65.94 (7.77)	61.92 (8.10)	66.43 (6.45)	3.493	.034*
OCB	92.21 (13.61)	89.18 (14.38)	94.50 (12.21)	.039	.962	96.93 (12.20)	89.46 (15.53)	92.57 (18.04)	3.709	.028*

* Denotes significant at 5% level

In case of Psychological contract (PC), it can be concluded that even at 5% level of significance there is no significant difference between the educational background of employees (f = 0.355, p = 0.701) and managers (f = 0.868, p = 0.422) towards psychological contract.

In case of Psychological empowerment (PE), it can be concluded that even at 5% level of significance there is no significant difference between the educational background of employees (f = 0.069, p = 0.933) and managers (f = 0.076, p = 0.927) towards the psychological empowerment.

In case of Employee involvement (EI), it can be concluded that even at 5% level of significance there is no significant difference between the educational background of employees (f = 0.138, p = 0.871) and managers (f = 0.884, p = 0.416) towards the involvement.

In case of Cultural Intelligence (CI), it can be concluded that even at 5% level of significance there is no significant difference between the educational background of employees (f = 0.107, p = 0.898) and managers (f = 0.177, p = 0.838) towards the level of cultural knowledge.

In case of Psychological ownership (PO), it can be concluded that even at 5% level of significance there is no significant difference between the educational background of employees (f = 0.838, p = 0.434) and managers (f = 1.980, p = 0.143) towards the behavior at their work place.

In case of Organisational support (OS), it can be concluded that even at 5% level of significance there is no significant difference between the educational background of employees (f = 0.274, p = 0.760) and managers (f = 1.158, p = 0.318) towards the organisational support received from their banks.

In case of In role performance (IRP), it can be concluded that even at 5% level of significance there is no significant difference between the educational background of employees (f = 0.954, p = 0.387) and there is a significant difference between the educational background of managers (f = 4.167, p = 0.018) towards their level of performance at work.

In case of Psychological well-being (PW), it can be concluded that even at 5% level of significance there is no significant difference between the educational background of employees (f =1.030, p = 0.359) and managers (f = 1.616, p = 0.203) towards the well-being perceived from both work and from personal.

In case of Organisational commitment (OC), it can be concluded that even at 5% level of significance there is no significant difference between the educational background of employees (f = 1.834, p = 0.162) and there is a significant difference between the educational background of managers (f = 3.493, p = 0.034) towards their level of commitment to complete their organisational task.

In case of Organisational citizenship behavior (OCB), it can be concluded that even at 5% level of significance there is no significant difference between the educational background of employees (f = 0.039, p = 0.962) and there is a significant difference between the educational background of managers (f = 3.709, p = 0.028) towards the behavior at their work place.

Results of ANOVA for Educational Background, ERM Dimensions PW, OC and OCB:

The ANOVA results explain that there is no significant difference between employees and managers level of education with regards to PC, PE, EI, CI, PO, POS and PW, whereas, in case of manager IRP OC and OCB was influenced by various levels of education. Further PG background manager's mean score was comparatively low with UG and other educational background managers. This may be because newly promoted manager with PG background have higher performance competition where they need to be more committed, which in-turn helps them to behave as a good organisational citizen.

The findings of ANOVA was supported by Bakan, Buyukbese and Ersahan (2011) in which they concluded that there is a significant relationship between level of education and organisational commitment.

Hypotheses - 6

There is no significant difference between gender and ERM Dimensions and PW, OC, OCB for Employees and Managers.

Table 4.3.5.4   T Test for Gender, ERM Dimensions, PW, OC and OCB.

IV & DV	Employee				Manager			
	Gender		T value	P value	Gender		T value	P value
	Male	Female			Male	Female		
PC	137.53 (18.96)	140.80 (17.67)	1.413	0.159	151.75 (14.03)	152.58 (12.48)	0.239	0.811
PE	45.96 (5.98)	46.27 (5.41)	0.435	0.664	49.10 (5.05)	49.89 (5.80)	0.608	0.544
EI	44.86 (8.56)	46.38 (8.06)	1.445	0.150	48.90 (7.53)	47.74 (9.04)	0.592	0.555
CI	69.24 (13.35)	69.70 (11.86)	0.289	0.773	73.06 (11.43)	75.68 (10.77)	0.921	0.359
PO	27.11 (5.19)	28.14 (4.54)	1.666	0.097	30.09 (4.80)	30.47 (4.61)	0.317	0.752
OS	26.84 (4.78)	28.06 (5.23)	1.921	0.056	29.18 (4.54)	30.00 (4.78)	0.716	0.475
IRP	25.10 (3.90)	26.28 (3.52)	2.507	0.013*	27.22 (3.32)	27.11 (3.16)	0.137	0.891

Table 4.3.5.4   *(Contd.)*

IV & DV	Employee				Manager			
	Gender		T value	P value	Gender		T value	P value
	Male	Female			Male	Female		
PW	208.82 (25.24)	207.72 (22.83)	0.361	0.718	215.25 (24.03)	216.95 (28.06)	0.274	0.785
OC	62.71 (8.25)	63.13 (7.55)	0.419	0.676	63.95 (8.25)	67.95 (5.53)	2.021	0.046*
OCB	90.81 (14.17)	91.74 (13.58)	0.531	0.596	93.95 (14.19)	95.05 (13.95)	0.311	0.756

* Denotes significant at 5% level

In case of Psychological contract (PC), it can be concluded that even at 5% level of significance there is no significant difference between the gender composition of employees ($f = 1.413$, $p = 0.159$) and managers ($f = 0.239$, $p = 0.811$) towards psychological contract.

In case of Psychological empowerment (PE), it can be concluded that even at 5% level of significance there is no significant difference between the gender composition of employees ($f = 0.435$, $p = 0.664$) and managers ($f = 0.608$, $p = 0.544$) towards their psychological empowerment.

In case of Employee involvement (EI), it can be concluded that even at 5% level of significance there is no significant difference between the gender composition of employees ($f = 1.445$, $p = 0.150$) and managers ($f = 0.592$, $p = 0.555$) towards the level of involvement at their work.

In case of Cultural Intelligence (CI), it can be concluded that even at 5% level of significance there is no significant difference between the gender composition of employees ($f = 0.289$, $p = 0.773$) and managers ($f = 0.921$, $p = 0.359$) towards the level of cultural knowledge.

In case of Psychological ownership (PO), it can be concluded that even at 5% level of significance there is no significant difference between the gender composition of employees ($f = 1.666$, $p = 0.097$) and managers ($f = 0.317$, $p = 0.752$) towards the psychological ownership feeling about their banks.

In case of Organisational support (OS), it can be concluded that even at 5% level of significance there is no significant difference between the gender composition of employees ($f = 1.921$, $p = 0.056$) and managers ($f = 0.716$, $p = 0.475$) towards the organisational support received from their superiors.

In case of In role performance (IRP), it can be concluded that even at 5% level of significance there is a significant difference between the gender composition of employees ($f = 2.507$, $p = 0.013$) and there is no significant difference between the educational background of managers ($f = 0.137$, $p = 0.891$) towards their performance.

In case of Psychological well-being (PW), it can be concluded that even at 5% level of significance there is no significant difference between the gender composition of employees ($f = 0.361$, $p = 0.718$) and managers ($f = 0.274$, $p = 0.785$) towards the well-being perceived from both work and from personal.

In case of Organisational commitment (OC), it can be concluded that even at 5% level of significance there is no significant difference between the gender composition of employees ($f = 0.419$, $p = 0.676$) and there is a significant difference between gender composition of managers ($f = 2.021$, $p = 0.046$) towards his/her commitment to complete their organisational task.

In case of Organisational citizenship behavior (OCB), it can be concluded that even at 5% level of significance there is no significant difference between the gender composition of employees ($f = 0.531$, $p = 0.596$) and managers ($f = 0.311$, $p = 0.756$) towards their work place behavior.

Results of Gender Composition, ERM Dimensions, Individual Well-Being and Work Place Behavior

The t test result shows that there is no significant difference between employees and managers gender composition with respect to certain ERM dimension, PW and OCB. As far as the gender composition of the ERM is concerned, both male and female individuals in the bank are having more or less the same perception about PC, PE, EI, CI, PO, POS, PW and OCB; whereas, there is a significant differences between employees IRP and managers OC. In these cases mean score of female respondents is higher than male respondents. This may be due to female employees working in the public sector bank performing better than that of male employees. Likewise, female managers are more committed than male managers.

This finding was supported by Rosa, Carter and Hamilton (1996) in which they finalized that gender appears to be a significant determinant towards performance. Further, this study was also supported by Kidder (2002) in which they demonstrated that there is a relationship between gender and the performance and OCB.

Hypotheses-7

There is no significant difference between marital status and ERM dimensions and PW, OC, OCB for employees and managers.

Table 4.3.5.5   T Test for Marital Status, ERM Dimensions, PW, OC and OCB.

IV & DV	Employees				Managers			
	Marital status		T value	P value	Marital status		T value	P value
	Married	Un married			Married	Un married		
PC	138.33 (18.47)	142.85 (17.47)	1.585	0.114	151.43 (13.21)	158.00 (19.63)	1.309	0.193
PE	46.00 (5.47)	46.60 (6.43)	0.673	0.501	49.00 (5.04)	52.38 (6.16)	1.801	0.074
EI	45.56 (8.15)	46.10 (8.99)	0.412	0.680	49.07 (7.19)	43.88 (13.14)	1.841	0.068
CI	68.76 (12.40)	72.25 (12.87)	1.793	0.074	72.72 (11.10)	83.88 (9.43)	2.765	0.007**
PO	27.91 (4.78)	26.69 (5.13)	1.609	0.109	30.22 (4.76)	29.25 (4.89)	0.557	0.578

Table 4.3.5.5 *(Contd.)*

IV & DV	Employees				Managers			
	Marital status		T value	P value	Marital status		T value	P value
	Married	Un married			Married	Un married		
OS	27.34 (4.86)	28.04 (5.73)	0.883	0.378	29.45 (4.39)	27.50 (6.61)	1.166	0.246
IRP	25.75 (3.82)	25.63 (3.43)	0.202	0.840	27.25 (3.24)	26.50 (3.96)	0.625	0.533
PW	208.06 (23.69)	208.90 (25.12)	0.226	0.822	214.84 (24.23)	224.75 (29.43)	1.099	0.274
OC	63.16 (7.54)	62.06 (9.05)	0.899	0.369	64.12 (7.80)	71.13 (8.11)	2.443	0.016*
OCB	91.17 (13.29)	91.83 (15.91)	0.303	0.762	93.11 (13.62)	107.75 (14.03)	2.926	0.004**

** Denotes significant at 1% level. 2. * Denotes significant at 5% level

In case of Psychological contract (PC), it can be concluded that even at 5% level of significance there is no significant difference between the marital status of employees (f = 1.585, p = 0.114) and managers (f = 1.309, p = 0.193) towards psychological contract.

In case of Psychological empowerment (PE), it can be concluded that even at 5% level of significance there is no significant difference between the marital status of employees (f = 0.673, p = 0.501) and managers (f = 1.801, p = 0.074) towards their psychological empowerment.

In case of Employee involvement (EI), it can be concluded that even at 5% level of significance there is no significant difference between the marital status of employees (f = 0.412, p = 0.680) and managers (f = 1.841, p = 0.068) towards the level of involvement at their work.

In case of Cultural Intelligence (CI), it can be concluded that even at 5% level of significance there is no significant difference between the marital status of employees (f = 1.793, p = 0.074) and at 1% level of significance there is a significant difference between marital status of managers (f = 2.765, p = 0.007) towards the cultural knowledge.

In case of Psychological ownership (PO), it can be concluded that even at 5% level of significance there is no significant difference between the marital status of employees (f = 1.609, p = 0.109) and managers (f = 0.557, p = 0.578) towards the psychological ownership.

In case of Organisational support (OS), it can be concluded that even at 5% level of significance there is no significant difference between the marital status of employees (f = 0.883, p = 0.378) and managers (f = 1.166, p = 0.246) towards the organisational support.

In case of In role performance (IRP), it can be concluded that even at 5% level of significance there is no significant difference between the marital status of employees (f = 0.202, p = 0.840) and managers (f = 0.625, p = 0.533) towards their level of performance at their work.

In case of Psychological well-being (PW), it can be concluded that even at 5% level of significance there is no significant difference between the marital status of employees (f = 0.226, p = 0.822) and managers (f = 1.099, p = 0.274) towards the well-being perceived from both work and from personal.

In case of Organisational commitment (OC), it can be concluded that even at 5% level of significance there is no significant difference between the marital status of employees (f = 0.899, p = 0.369) and there is a significant difference between marital status of managers (f = 2.443, p = 0.016) towards his/her commitment to complete their organisational task.

In case of Organisational citizenship behavior (OCB), it can be concluded that even at 5% level of significance there is no significant difference between the marital status of employees (f = 0.303, p = 0.762) and at 1% level of significance there is a significant difference between marital status of managers (f = 2.926, p = 0.004) towards their work place behavior.

Results of Marital status, ERM Dimensions, Individual Well-Being and Work Place Behavior

The t test results indicate that there is no significant difference between employee's marital status on ERM dimensions, PW, OC and OCB. In case of managers there is a significant difference between marital status on CI, OC and OCB. The mean score of married and unmarried employees are similar; therefore, there is no significant difference between ERM dimensions, individual well-being dimensions, OCB and marital status. But in case of managers CI, OC and OCB the mean score of unmarried is higher than married managers. This may be because the married managers have additional responsibilities towards their family.

These findings were supported by Qureshi et.al., (2012), in which they found the strong impact of marital status towards the organisational commitment.

Hypotheses – 8

There is no significant difference between work experience and ERM Dimensions and PW, OC, OCB for Employees and Managers.

Table 4.3.5.6 Anova for Experience, ERM Dimensions, PW, OC And OCB.

IV	Employees						Manager					
	Work experience in years				F value	P value	Work experience in years				F value	P value
	Below 10	11- 20	21 - 30	Above 30			Below 10	11- 20	21 - 30	Above 30		
PC	138.03 (19.76)	142.51 (19.04)	137.88 (15.97)	140.43 (18.26)	.778	.507	144.88 (9.45)	148.13 (10.08)	153.31 (15.76)	152.98 (13.55)	1.326	.270
PE	46.69 (5.82)	46.67 (6.56)	45.62 (4.63)	45.42 (5.89)	.871	.457	51.63 (5.63)	49.40 (5.97)	49.11 (5.11)	48.93 (4.96)	.643	.589
EI	46.09 (8.86)	47.30 (8.26)	44.40 (7.98)	45.30 (7.81)	1.194	.313	44.13 (8.44)	50.47 (7.03)	50.29 (7.42)	47.91 (7.89)	1.908	.132
CI	69.60 (14.04)	71.47 (13.07)	69.69 (10.59)	67.42 (11.93)	.844	.471	76.25 (11.30)	73.67 (9.78)	73.60 (13.48)	73.00 (10.46)	.192	.902
PO	27.49 (5.26)	26.79 (5.37)	28.18 (4.30)	27.96 (4.48)	.814	.487	27.13 (4.49)	30.33 (5.15)	30.23 (5.20)	30.49 (4.36)	1.194	.316

Table 4.3.5.6 (*Contd.*)

IV	Employees						Manager					
	Work experience in years				F value	P value	Work experience in years				F value	P value
	Below 10	11-20	21-30	Above 30			Below 10	11-20	21-30	Above 30		
OS	27.88 (5.35)	27.51 (5.39)	27.43 (4.75)	26.91 (4.71)	.412	.745	28.50 (3.63)	29.00 (3.16)	30.06 (4.94)	29.05 (4.79)	.473	.702
IRP	25.85 (3.70)	25.40 (4.25)	25.57 (3.60)	26.00 (3.61)	.273	.845	25.38 (4.00)	28.33 (3.99)	26.60 (3.22)	27.53 (2.90)	2.060	.110
PW	207.73 (26.20)	209.51 (25.54)	207.57 (22.40)	208.87 (21.15)	.082	.970	222.25 (19.03)	207.00 (31.99)	217.14 (26.84)	215.84 (21.61)	.849	.470
OC	62.07 (7.39)	64.09 (9.20)	63.41 (8.24)	62.77 (7.01)	.744	.526	65.63 (5.63)	62.33 (8.32)	64.91 (8.66)	64.88 (7.84)	.481	.696
OCB	92.79 (13.16)	91.09 (15.39)	91.72 (14.56)	88.55 (12.58)	1.056	.368	97.50 (12.39)	90.33 (18.08)	94.09 (15.21)	94.68 (12.54)	.538	.657

In case of Psychological contract (PC), it can be concluded that even at 5% level of significance there is no significant difference between the experience of employees (f = 0.778, p = 0.507) and managers (f = 1.326, p = 0.270) towards psychological contract.

In case of Psychological empowerment (PE), it can be concluded that even at 5% level of significance there is no significant difference between the experience of employees (f = 0.871, p = 0.457) and managers (f = 0.643, p = 0.589) towards psychological empowerment.

In case of Employee involvement (EI), it can be concluded that even at 5% level of significance there is no significant difference between the experience of employees (f = 1.194, p = 0.313) and managers (f = 1.908, p = 0.132) towards employee involvement.

In case of Cultural Intelligence (CI), it can be concluded that even at 5% level of significance there is no significant difference between the experience of employees (f = 0.844, p = 0.471) and managers (f = 0.192, p = 0.902) towards level of cultural knowledge.

In case of Psychological ownership (PO), it can be concluded that even at 5% level of significance there is no significant difference between the experience of employees (f = 0.814, p = 0.487) and managers (f = 1.194, p = 0.316) towards the psychological ownership.

In case of Organisational support (OS), it can be concluded that even at 5% level of significance there is no significant difference between the experience of employees (f = 0.412, p = 0.745) and managers (f = 0.473, p = 0.702) towards the organisational support received from their superiors to attain their task.

In case of In role performance (IRP), it can be concluded that even at 5% level of significance there is no significant difference between the experience of employees (f = 0.273, p = 0.845) and managers (f = 2.060, p = 0.110) towards the in role performance.

In case of Psychological well-being (PW), it can be concluded that even at 5% level of significance there is no significant difference between the experience of employees (f = 0.082, p = 0.970) and managers (f = 0.849, p = 0.470) towards their personal and organisational well-being.

In case of Organisational commitment (OC), it can be concluded that even at 5% level of significance there is no significant difference between the experience of employees (f = 0.744, p = 0.526) and managers (f = 0.481, p = 0.696) towards level of commitment.

In case of Organisational citizenship behavior (OCB), it can be concluded that even at 5% level of significance there is no significant difference between the experience of employees (f = 1.056, p = 0.368) and managers (f = 0.538, p = 0.657) towards their work place behavior.

Results of ERM Dimensions, PW, OC, OCB and Experience

The findings of the one way ANOVA explain that there is no significant difference between work experience of employees and managers towards ERM dimensions, PW, OC and OCB. The mean score of variables were similar and it shows that employees and managers perceptions towards these variables are not influenced by their work experience. This may be due to that employees and managers working in the public sector banks work together as a team to serve their customers.

4.3.6   TO FIND OUT THE ASSOCIATION BETWEEN EMPLOY-EES AND MANAGERS JOB SATISFACTION AND HAPPI-NESS PERCEIVED FROM THEIR WORK.

Hypotheses-9

There will be significant association between Happiness and Job satisfaction.

Table 4.3.6 Chi-Square Test for Happiness and Job Satisfaction

Happiness	Job satisfaction						Chi square value		P value		Phi Cramer's V Contingency Coefficient	
	Employees			Manager			Employees	Manager	Employees	Manager	Employees	Manager
	Yes	No	Total	Yes	No	Total						
Yes	199	25	224	91	13	104	61.581	12.751	0.000	.003	0.000	.001
No	7	19	26	6	6	11						
Total	206	44	250	96	19	115						

The above table explains the results for the Continuity correction, in case of employees it shows that (1) = 61.581, p = <0.000 and in case of managers it is (1) = 12.571, p = 0.003. Therefore the chi-square test proved that there is a significant association between Happiness and Job satisfaction.

Thus happiness quotient of bank employees as well as managers were quite high; further this make them to feel satisfied in their Job. Phi and Cramer's V are both tests of the strength of association which shows that the strength of association between the variables is very strong. The asymptotic significance in the test statistics is 0.001 which is less than 0.01. Hence null hypothesis is rejected and research hypothesis is accepted; therefore, there is a significance association between "Happiness and Job satisfaction".

4.3.7 TO ANALYZE THE SIGNIFICANT DIFFERENCE BE-TWEEN EMPLOYEES AND MANAGER'S FRIENDLY RE-LATIONSHIP BASED ON THEIR AGE.

Hypotheses-10

There is a significant difference in the friendly relationship among employees in public sector banks based on their age.

Table 4.3.7   Anova for Age Group and Friendly Relationship.

Friendly relationship		Age Group in years				F	Sig.
		Below 30	31-40	41-50	Above 50		
Do you have friends at your work place?	Employee	2.12 (0.569)	2.30 (0.950)	2.00 (0.000)	1.01 (0.113)	1.819	.096
	Manager	1.40 (0.548)	2.14 (0.378)	2.00 (0.000)	1.05 (0.206)	2.724	.023*

The above table shows the output of the ANOVA and explains that p value in case of employees is 0.096 which is more than 5% level, therefore, null hypotheses is accepted. There is no statistical significant difference in friendly relationship and age level of employees working in public sector banks; whereas, p value in case of managers is 0.023

which is less than 5% level. Therefore, research hypotheses was accepted. There is a statisticaly significant difference between friendly relationship and age level of managers working in public sector banks.

4.3.8   TO DETERMINE FACTORS INFLUENCING EMPLOYEE RELATIONSHIP MANAGEMENT (ERM).

Employee relationship management is the employment relations between employees and managers working in leading public sector banks. Factor analysis was performed to find the dimensions and also to find most predominant factor influencing the managers and employees towards their employment. Psychological contract, psychological empowerment, psychological well being, psychological ownership, cultural intelligence, organisational commitment, organisational support, organisational citizenship behavior, employee involvement and in role performance and its dimensions were taken and assumed as the dimensions of ERM.

4.3.8.1   *Managers Perspective*

KMO and Bartlett's Test

Kaiser-Meyer-Olkin (KMO) Measure of Sampling Adequacy/ Bartlett's Test of Sphericity. Prior to the extraction of the factors, several tests are required to be used to assess the suitability of the respondent data for factor analysis. These tests include Kaiser-Meyer-Olkin (KMO) Measure of Sampling Adequacy, and Bartlett's Test of Sphericity.

Table 4.3.8.1.1   KMO and Bartlett's Test

Kaiser-Meyer-Olkin Measure of Sampling Adequacy.		.772
Bartlett's Test of Sphericity	Approx. Chi-Square	5430.200
	df	1540
	Sig.	.000

The Kaiser-Meyer-Olkin Measure of Sampling Adequacy is a statistics that indicates the proportion of variance in variables that might be caused by underlying factors. In this study, the value of Kaiser-Meyer-Olkin Measure of Sampling Adequacy is 0.772. Bartlett's tests the hypothesis that correlation matrix is an identity matrix, which would indicate that variables are unrelated and therefore unsuitable for structure detection. A small value (less than 0.05) of the significance level indicates that a factor analysis may be useful with data.

Table 4.3.8.1.2   Communalities

	Initial	Extraction
Performance support 1	1.000	.623
Performance support 2	1.000	.804
Performance support 3	1.000	.818
Performance support 4	1.000	.781
Employee development 1	1.000	.778
Employee development 2	1.000	.643
Employee development 3	1.000	.640
Meaning 1	1.000	.696
Meaning 2	1.000	.708
Meaning 3	1.000	.720
Impact 1	1.000	.618
Job satisfaction 1	1.000	.547
Job satisfaction 2	1.000	.553
Job satisfaction 11	1.000	.601
Intrinsic job motivation 2	1.000	.587
Intrinsic job motivation 4	1.000	.724
Intrinsic job motivation 5	1.000	.732
Intrinsic job motivation 6	1.000	.707
High order need 3	1.000	.591
High order need 4	1.000	.704
Perceived intrinsic job characteristics 2	1.000	.711
Perceived intrinsic job characteristics 3	1.000	.681
Perceived intrinsic job characteristics 4	1.000	.575
Perceived intrinsic job characteristics 6	1.000	.612
Life satisfaction 8	1.000	.694
Life satisfaction 9	1.000	.820

	Initial	Extraction
Life satisfaction 10	1.000	.843
Happiness	1.000	.711
Self rate danxiety 6	1.000	.569
Information 1	1.000	.690
Information 2	1.000	.798
Information 3	1.000	.693
Reward 2	1.000	.809
Knowledge 1	1.000	.697
Metacognitive 2	1.000	.809
Metacognitive 3	1.000	.765
Metacognitive 4	1.000	.799
Motivational 2	1.000	.773
Motivational 3	1.000	.735
Behavioral 1	1.000	.760
Behavioral 3	1.000	.780
Behavioral 4	1.000	.779
Psychological ownership 1	1.000	.721
Psychological ownership 3	1.000	.822
Psychological ownership 4	1.000	.796
Psychological ownership 5	1.000	.843
Organisational support 1	1.000	.734
Organisational support 2	1.000	.749
Organisational support 3	1.000	.751
Organisational support 4	1.000	.669
Altruism 4	1.000	.751
Altruism 5	1.000	.702
Courtesy 1	1.000	.590
Civicvirtue 2	1.000	.713
Civicvirtue 3	1.000	.708
Civicvirtue 4	1.000	.654

Extraction Method: Principal Component Analysis.

Communalities indicate the amount of variance in each variable by the extracted factors. Initial communalities are estimates of the variance in each variable accounted by all components or factors. Extraction communalities are the squared multiple correlation coefficient obtained by using all of the factors to predict each item score in-turn. For instance, .843 for psychological ownership5 means that 84.3% of the variance in this item is explained by all of the factors produced in this analysis and .547 for Job satisfaction1 explains that 54.7% of the variance in this item is explained by all factors produced.

FACTOR ANALYSIS

Factor analysis is used in data reduction to identify number of factors that explain most of the variance observed in a much larger number of manifest variables. The loadings of the item in factor explain the correlation between item and that factor. An eigenvalue for a Factor is obtained by squaring the every item on that factor, and adding these squared factor loadings together. In this study factor analysis is performed to analyze the manager's perceptions towards ERM and accordingly the results are as follows.

Table 4.3.8.1.3   Total Variance Explained

Component	Initial Eigen values			Extraction Sums of Squared Loadings			Rotation Sums of Squared Loadings		
	Total	% of Variance	Cumulative %	Total	% of Variance	Cumulative %	Total	% of Variance	Cumulative %
1	15.267	27.262	27.262	15.267	27.262	27.262	6.920	12.357	12.357
2	5.254	9.382	36.644	5.254	9.382	36.644	5.013	8.952	21.309
3	3.640	6.500	43.144	3.640	6.500	43.144	4.525	8.080	29.389
4	3.294	5.882	49.027	3.294	5.882	49.027	3.923	7.005	36.394
5	2.640	4.715	53.741	2.640	4.715	53.741	3.892	6.949	43.343
6	2.482	4.432	58.173	2.482	4.432	58.173	3.691	6.591	49.934
7	2.085	3.723	61.896	2.085	3.723	61.896	3.292	5.878	55.812
8	1.829	3.266	65.162	1.829	3.266	65.162	3.101	5.537	61.349
9	1.768	3.157	68.319	1.768	3.157	68.319	3.018	5.390	66.739
10	1.625	2.902	71.221	1.625	2.902	71.221	2.510	4.482	71.221

Extraction Method: Principal Component Analysis.

ROTATED COMPONENT MATRIX

The most important tool in interpreting factors is factor rotation. The term rotation means the reference axes of the factors are turned about the origin until some other position had been reached. Factor rotation assists in the interpretation of the factors by simplifying the structure through maximizing the significant loadings of a variable on a single factor.

Table 4.3.8.1.4   Rotated Component Matrix[a]

	Component									
	1	2	3	4	5	6	7	8	9	10
Reward 2	.819	.092	.109	.050	-.025	.328	-.053	.028	-.053	.023
Organisational support 3	.755	-.127	.227	.021	.094	.151	.226	.054	-.139	.087
Organisational support 1	.748	-.146	.180	.109	.096	.057	.299	.079	-.023	-.006
Knowledge1	.745	.017	.191	.101	.035	.212	-.060	.118	-.041	.171
Perceived intrinsic job characteristics 3	.709	.253	-.089	.117	.121	.009	-.086	-.015	.184	.190
Organisational support 2	.698	.005	.228	-.102	.035	.242	.373	-.026	.018	.001
Organisational support 4	.663	.184	-.074	.081	-.076	.355	.119	.143	.133	.022
Information 3	.631	.040	.238	-.039	.189	.001	-.072	.139	.243	.341
Jobsatisfaction 1	.629	.237	.167	.162	.085	.018	-.131	-.110	-.012	.062
Jobsatisfaction 11	.612	.329	.018	.123	-.105	.034	.135	-.237	.124	-.033

	Component									
	1	2	3	4	5	6	7	8	9	10
Perceived intrinsic job characteristics 4	.542	-.040	.156	.403	.039	-.099	.197	.072	.080	.176
Courtesy 1	.496	.174	-.076	.191	.167	.219	.222	.093	.369	.041
Performance support 3	.014	.834	.149	.029	.086	.066	.064	.184	-.066	.213
Performance support 4	.034	.809	.143	.032	.150	-.003	.079	.218	-.002	.165
Performance support 2	-.036	.805	.052	.107	.008	-.079	.156	.203	-.040	.257
Employee development 1	.230	.775	.069	.222	.195	.065	-.001	.023	.131	-.102
Employee development 2	.157	.678	.106	.091	.093	.151	-.018	.027	.296	-.141
Employee development 3	.166	.655	.208	.112	.130	.113	.026	-.017	.258	-.173
Performance support 1	.078	.581	.091	.305	.224	.080	.184	.162	.214	.125
Psychological ownership 4	.158	.155	.843	.077	.123	.069	.013	.027	.101	-.009
Psychological ownership 5	.181	.145	.838	.045	.140	.153	.124	.041	.153	.054
Psychological ownership 3	.223	.148	.818	.110	.153	.067	.134	.097	.106	.052
Psychological ownership 1	.139	.204	.790	.041	.036	.143	.045	.036	-.006	.100
Meaning 2	.166	.003	.537	.273	-.033	-.041	.487	-.055	.071	.265
Meaning 3	.069	-.002	.527	.318	-.073	.069	.500	-.024	.122	.246
Intrinsic job motivation 5	.054	.144	.019	.798	-.007	.090	.169	-.118	-.042	.139

	Component									
	1	2	3	4	5	6	7	8	9	10
High order need 4	.348	.103	-.039	.680	-.001	-.055	-.122	.284	.100	-.009
Intrinsic job motivation 4	-.055	.257	.099	.618	.115	.227	.387	-.067	.002	.209
Intrinsic job motivation 2	.049	.042	.367	.589	-.069	.176	.203	.113	.085	.058
High order need 3	.290	.263	.126	.588	.155	.109	.044	-.061	.116	-.143
Intrinsic job motivation 6	-.092	.301	.264	.570	.161	.156	.171	-.131	.286	.188
Perceived intrinsic job characteristics 2	.421	.037	.098	.535	.121	.110	-.211	.020	.388	-.122
Job satisfaction 2	.436	.011	-.009	.494	.024	.204	-.210	-.003	.024	.179
Metacognitive 2	.019	.114	.176	.095	.849	.090	.127	.064	.042	.068
Metacognitive 4	.044	.151	.010	.018	.834	.105	.129	.190	-.002	.119
Metacognitive 3	.043	.128	.182	.004	.827	.039	.099	.075	.073	.087
Motivational 3	.160	.144	-.021	.052	.685	-.022	.085	.400	.215	.051
Motivational 2	.181	.212	.055	.071	.643	-.019	.019	.453	.221	.137
Life satisfaction 10	.178	.058	.122	.157	.056	.852	.030	.125	.144	-.041
Life satisfaction 9	.113	-.030	.126	.042	.011	.838	.167	.042	-.232	-.061
Life satisfaction 8	.268	.063	.060	.087	-.022	.743	-.040	.155	-.023	.167
Happiness	.285	.088	.077	.135	.121	.720	.129	.010	.193	.110
Self rate danxiety 6	.168	.179	.185	.139	.203	.532	.059	-.065	.156	.314

	Component									
	1	2	3	4	5	6	7	8	9	10
Civicvirtue 2	.168	.088	.108	.013	.109	.144	.786	.094	-.034	.066
Civicvirtue 3	.103	.209	.195	.096	.232	.117	.673	.055	.280	-.070
Civicvirtue 4	.046	.091	.082	.120	.248	.025	.671	.196	.267	-.005
Behavioral 3	-.007	.142	-.114	-.003	.163	.100	.170	.825	.026	-.001
Behavioral 4	.012	.212	.115	-.001	.224	.099	.031	.811	.020	-.040
Behavioral 1	.071	.156	.184	-.023	.272	.124	.054	.768	.112	.041
Altruism 4	.079	.183	.176	.054	-.017	-.131	.278	.325	.670	.167
Impact 1	.055	.142	.083	.095	.169	.127	.002	-.121	.664	.281
Meaning 1	-.038	.071	.460	.094	.147	.090	.143	.040	.646	.015
Altruism 5	.108	.214	.015	.183	.109	-.056	.366	.287	.588	.186
Information 2	.243	.012	.209	.037	.135	.211	.018	.110	.268	.739
Information 1	.148	.238	.175	.129	.099	.077	.042	-.048	.209	.708
Perceived intrinsic job characteristics 6	.356	.032	-.058	.189	.252	.036	.148	.004	-.009	.599

Extraction Method: Principal Component Analysis.
Rotation Method: Varimax with Kaiser Normalization.
a. Rotation converged in 8 iterations.

Table 4.3.8.1.5   Reliability Statistics

Cronbach's Alpha	N of Items
.949	56

The rotated component matrix table shows the loadings of each item on each factor after rotation. The rotated component factor has combined the 56 statements into ten factors with the reliability of 94.9% and on the basis of loading of the statements they are given names and explained below.

FACTOR–1 ENGAGEMENT FACTOR

Following are the major statements loaded in this factor.

- I am satisfied with recognition received for doing a good job
- My bank strongly considers my goals and values.
- My bank cares about my opinions.
- I am given a real opportunity to improve my skills at bank
- My bank really cares about my well-being.
- Help is available from my superiors when I had a problem.
- I am recognized for my good work
- My superiors give a clear picture of banking strategy
- I'm satisfied with the physical work conditions
- I am satisfied with my bank environment.
- I am able to judge my work performance, right away, when actually doing the job
- I consider the impact of his or her actions on colleagues.

Managers are in agreement that contemporary or modern business focus on higher efficiency, than in older times. Organisations are trying to increase their performance in order to place their company ahead of its competitors. In the earlier days and even in today's context satisfied employees who are contented with their job will give competitive edge to the firm. A satisfied employee who wanted to be committed and stay with the company, contributed to the workforce solidity and productivity.

FACTOR–2 TALENT MANAGEMENT:

Major statements loaded in the factors are as follows.

- I will respond positively to dynamic performance requirements.

- I will accept new and different performance demands.

- I will adjust to changing performance demands due to business necessity.

- I seek out developmental opportunities that enhance my value to this bank.

- I build skills to increase my value to this bank.

- I make myself increasingly valuable to my bank.

- I will accept increasingly challenging performance standards.

Organisations revolve around people starting from identifying, recruiting, and selecting till the placement of employees. The art of managing the facet of people that includes development, performance engagement, rewarding, recognition, succession planning falls under the Talent management banner.

FACTOR-3 PERSONAL SATISFACTION:

Major statements loaded in this factor are as follows

- I sense that this Bank belonged to ME

- This is OUR Bank

- I feel a very high degree of personal ownership for this Bank.

- This is MY Bank.

- My job activities are personally meaningful to me.

- The work I do is meaningful to me.

Managers are strategically placed in the organisation hierarchy to ensure that the business functions smoothly. More often than not the authority is used in a manner to constrict its subordinates. Therefore they should understand where they fit into and what they do will be ultimately affect or effect in business. Feeling of possession and meaningfulness in job increase the individual satisfaction in an organisation. Satisfaction of employees form an integral part of the business function and this faction has to be managed carefully.

FACTOR-4 ORGANISATIONAL WELL BEING

Following are the major statements loaded in this factor.

- I like to look back on the day's work with a sense of a job well done

- I am having enough opportunity to learn new things

- I feel unhappy when my work is not up to my usual standard

- My opinion of myself goes down when I do this job badly

- I am having enough opportunity to make my own decisions

- I try to think of ways of doing my job effectively

- I am satisfied with the amount of responsibility given to me to perform my job

- I had freedom to choose my own method of working

Performance is largely linked to the surrounding. A serene work environment with all the basic needs help people to perform at higher levels. An organisation that gives importance toward well being is found to be placed in a better position than organisation who only focus on business and not the well being aspect. Wellbeing faction creates a wonderful work environment that results in people knowing what they do and perform beyond ones potential. To understand and thrust the need for belongingness, an employer (Organisation) can align many tasks to its employees during the orientation process or even handle tasks that are challenging in nature that involves a certain degree of decision making.

FACTOR-5 CULTURAL INTELLIGENCE:

Major statements loaded in this factor are as follows.

- I adjust my cultural knowledge as I interact with people from a culture that is unfamiliar to me.

- I check the accuracy of my cultural knowledge as I interact with people from different cultures.

- I am conscious of the cultural knowledge I apply to cross-cultural interactions.

- I am sure I can deal with the stresses of adjusting to a culture that is new to me.

- I am confident that I can socialize with locals in a culture that is unfamiliar to me.

In today's linguistic world managers need to be forthcoming in doing business with people from all kinds of cultures—both within their immediate geography and outside. This global connect has only made the business more challenging and it is imperative for an employer to embrace wide variety of culture. The practice of being inclusive and appreciating cross border culture is called cultural intelligence.

FACTOR-6 PSYCHOLOGICAL WELLBEING

Following are the major statements loaded in this factor

- I'm satisfied with social life
- I'm satisfied with my family life

- Taking everything together, I'm satisfied in my life as a whole these days.

- Taking all things together I would say that I am very much happy these days.

Social and life satisfaction play a vital role in every organisation. Thought preludes thought and so it preludes judgment. Thinking power is a gift that man possesses and largely this sense is almost negligibly available in any other being. Psychological well-being, is a powerful factor that effects or affects business. A considerably large part of psychological well being is also connected to social life, professional life and family life.

FACTOR-7 ORGANISATIONAL CITIZENSHIP BEHAVIOR

Major statements loaded in this factor are as follows.

- I shall attend meetings that are NOT mandatory, but are considered important.

- I keep abreast of changes in the bank.

- I read and keep up with bank announcements, memos, and so on.

Organisational citizenship behavior (OCB) is optional for the employee's activity which is not explicitly part of the job description and tends to promote the organisation. Good behavior only promotes that individual further and somewhat influences the organisation to move ahead. So to speak a person displaying good behavior is a good influence amongst his/her peers and a person displaying improper behavior influences otherwise. Though the behavior is not a part of the official system and does not hold any rewards or compensation it is often a much talked about topic as to how things may turn for the worse within the team or organisation. Some of the attributes of an OCB included are sportsmanship, continued involvement in professional, social environment and the open arm acceptance of rules and regulations of an organisation.

FACTOR – 8 BEHAVIORAL

Major statements loaded in this factor are as follows.

- I change my verbal behavior (e.g., accent, tone) when a cross-cultural interaction requires it.

- I vary the rate of my speaking when a cross-cultural situation requires it.

- I change my non-verbal behavior when a cross-cultural situation requires it.

Attitude makes the difference. In an organisation there are only two types of people, one with a good and the other with a poor attitude. The stance that an individual takes beginning their attitude influences what, how, when, where and why they do. An individual with a good behavioral attitude enrich other person and an organisation with team of such employees enhance the growth of an organisation. Likewise a person with a poor attitude is as good as a bad apple and how they influence the surrounding will be best left unsaid. Good people with great attitude form a great team and thus a great organisation.

FACTOR-9 RESPONSIBILITY FACTOR

Major statements loaded in this factor are as follows

- I am always ready to lend a helping hand to those around me.

- My impact on what happens in my branch is large.

- The work that I do is important to me.

- I am willing to help others who had work related problems.

An organisation during a course of its growth and the time in business has a huge influence to its immediate surroundings, government and country as a whole. It is thus imperative and of greatest importance that the company does the right thing and is responsible to its act. As such the contemporary business has entered a global scene and with stakeholders everywhere the stakes of being responsible are high too. In addition to this financial well being of the company is also of high importance. A company whose financial health is good is often looked at as a progressive company and to a great extent influences investments at a global scene that pushes the country forward. An ethical employer does not think of employees only as a means to an end but the means itself and how one can mutually co-exist. People of the organisation must be treated as a major stakeholder group. Ethical employers constantly look for opportunities to treat its people better, protect them however possible and promote them as often as they can.

FACTOR – 10 INVOLVEMENT

Major statements loaded in this factor are as follows.

- I had enough information to do my job well

- The information systems I use are effective

- The amount of variety in my job makes me more interesting

Involvement like engagement refers to opportunities for employer/employee to take part in decisions that affect the government and/or business. An involved employer/employee is like a well-oiled wheel who progress himself ahead of their competitors with great excitement and enthusiasm. Involvement is often used synonymously with the term 'direct participation'.

4.3.8.2   *Employees perspective*

KMO and Bartlett's Test

Prior to the extraction of the factors, several tests should be used to assess the suitability of the respondent data for factor analysis. These tests include Kaiser-Meyer-Olkin (KMO) Measure of Sampling Adequacy, and Bartlett's Test of Sphericity.

Table 4.3.8.2.1   KMO and Bartlett's Test

Kaiser-Meyer-Olkin Measure of Sampling Adequacy.		.803
Bartlett's Test of Sphericity	Approx. Chi-Square	4494.292
	df	595
	Sig.	.000

The Kaiser-Meyer-Olkin Measure of Sampling Adequacy is a statistics that indicates the proportion of variance in variable that might be caused by underlying factors. High values (close to 1.0) generally indicate that a factor analysis may be useful with data. If the value is less than 0.50, the result of the factor analysis probably would not be very useful. In this study, the value of Kaiser-Meyer-Olkin Measure of Sampling Adequacy is 0.803. Bartlett's tests the hypothesis that correlation matrix is an identity matrix, which would indicate that variables are unrelated and therefore unsuitable for structure detection. A small value (less than 0.05) of the significance level indicates that a factor analysis may be useful with data.

Table 4.3.8.2.2   Communalities

	Initial	Extraction
Employee stability 1	1.000	.656
Employee stability 2	1.000	.503
Employee stability 3	1.000	.790
Employee stability 4	1.000	.606
Competence 1	1.000	.847
Competence 2	1.000	.868
Intrinsic job motivation 3	1.000	.702
Intrinsic job motivation 4	1.000	.695
Intrinsic job motivation 5	1.000	.720
Intrinsic job motivation 6	1.000	.686
High order need 4	1.000	.674
High order need 6	1.000	.726
Perceived intrinsic job characteristics 2	1.000	.636
Perceived intrinsic job characteristics 5	1.000	.641
Life satisfaction 7	1.000	.529
Life satisfaction 8	1.000	.740
Life satisfaction 9	1.000	.734
Life satisfaction 10	1.000	.766

	Initial	Extraction
Self rate danxiety 2	1.000	.668
Self rate danxiety 3	1.000	.819
Self rate danxiety 4	1.000	.812
Self rate danxiety 5	1.000	.560
Self rate danxiety 6	1.000	.667
Metacognitive 1	1.000	.771
Metacognitive 2	1.000	.845
Metacognitive 3	1.000	.858
Metacognitive 4	1.000	.643
Motivational 2	1.000	.801
Motivational 3	1.000	.794
In role performance 1	1.000	.701
In role performance 2	1.000	.855
In role performance 3	1.000	.828
Altruism 1	1.000	.559
Altruism 2	1.000	.767
Altruism 3	1.000	.697

Extraction Method: Principal Component Analysis.

Communalities indicate the amount of variance in each variable by the extracted factors. Initial communalities are estimates of the variance in each variable accounted by all components or factors. Extraction communalities are the squared multiple correlation coefficient obtained by using all of the factors to predict each item score in-turn. For instance, .868 for Competence2 means that 86.8% of the variance in this item is explained by all of the factors produced in this analysis. Likewise .502 for Employee stability 2 explains that 50.2% of the variance in this item is explained by all factors produced.

FACTOR ANALYSIS

The present study uses the factor analysis to analyze the employees perception towards ERM and the results were presented below.

Table 4.3.8.2.3 Total Variance Explained

Component	Initial Eigenvalues			Extraction Sums of Squared Loadings			Rotation Sums of Squared Loadings		
	Total	% of Variance	Cumulative %	Total	% of Variance	Cumulative %	Total	% of Variance	Cumulative %
1	7.631	21.803	21.803	7.631	21.803	21.803	3.334	9.525	9.525
2	2.969	8.484	30.287	2.969	8.484	30.287	3.076	8.788	18.313
3	2.629	7.511	37.798	2.629	7.511	37.798	2.816	8.045	26.358
4	2.369	6.769	44.566	2.369	6.769	44.566	2.779	7.941	34.298
5	2.028	5.795	50.362	2.028	5.795	50.362	2.591	7.401	41.700
6	1.782	5.092	55.453	1.782	5.092	55.453	2.583	7.380	49.080
7	1.669	4.767	60.220	1.669	4.767	60.220	2.468	7.052	56.132
8	1.488	4.251	64.472	1.488	4.251	64.472	2.046	5.846	61.978
9	1.364	3.898	68.370	1.364	3.898	68.370	1.751	5.003	66.981
10	1.232	3.520	71.890	1.232	3.520	71.890	1.718	4.908	71.890

Extraction Method: Principal Component Analysis.

Table shows that the factor appears in each row. The eigenvalue factor1 has a total of 7.631 and it is accounted for 21.803% of all variance in the items. 8.484% for factor 2, 7 and 3.520% for factor10. Overall 71.890% variance is accounted for and explained by all factors.

ROTATED COMPONENT MATRIX

Factor rotation assists in the interpretation of the factors by simplifying the structure through maximizing the significant loadings of a variable on a single factor.

Table 4.3.8.2.4   Rotated Component Matrix[a]

	Component									
	1	2	3	4	5	6	7	8	9	10
Life satisfaction 10	.839	.053	.113	.116	.027	.107	.114	.052	.071	.004
Life satisfaction 8	.838	.162	.074	.031	.004	.013	.036	.005	.050	.033
Life satisfaction 9	.815	.110	.085	-.055	.025	.027	.069	-.011	.202	-.015
Life satisfaction 7	.694	.106	.000	.067	.092	.101	.011	.082	-.028	.070
Self rate danxiety 6	.677	.100	.215	.323	.000	.196	.098	.022	-.008	-.017
Metacognitive 2	.117	.892	-.004	.136	.030	.050	.068	.055	.028	.064
Metacognitive 3	.156	.885	.095	.077	.074	.097	.097	.083	.031	.056
Metacognitive 1	.141	.844	.023	.121	.086	-.004	.077	.099	.003	.014
Metacognitive 4	.127	.681	.129	.105	.092	-.029	.126	-.083	.070	.315
Self rate danxiety 4	.092	.064	.869	-.026	.059	.122	.097	.096	.071	.046
Self rate danxiety 3	.076	.059	.838	.035	.230	.161	.119	.086	.033	.074
Self rate danxiety 2	.099	-.051	.767	.099	.194	.109	-.045	.026	-.017	-.071
Self rate danxiety 5	.132	.146	.679	.046	.010	.046	.198	.120	.040	-.029
High order need 6	.010	.109	.047	.832	.011	.083	.016	.064	.076	.049
High orderneed 4	-.001	.134	.045	.793	.009	.070	.090	.040	.099	-.018
Perceived intrinsic job characteristics 5	.182	.078	.017	.732	.141	.077	.182	.057	.004	-.065
Perceived intrinsic job characteristics 2	.166	.069	.026	.726	.061	.208	.127	-.096	-.003	-.054
Intrinsic job motivation 3	.062	.043	.110	.164	.785	.080	-.036	.081	.002	.161

	Component									
	1	2	3	4	5	6	7	8	9	10
Intrinsic job motivation 4	-.026	.137	.112	-.099	.772	.211	-.043	.071	-.055	-.051
Intrinsic job motivation 5	.120	.073	.127	.060	.769	.035	.187	.089	.209	.038
Intrinsic job motivation 6	.005	.021	.150	.114	.713	.030	.331	.029	.134	-.111
Employee stability 3	.010	-.013	.165	.100	.040	.856	.072	.052	.093	-.045
Employee stability 1	.095	-.017	.048	.063	.094	.779	.112	.098	.014	.050
Employee stability 4	.192	.129	.071	.085	.037	.726	.104	.032	.007	-.018
Employee stability 2	.063	.012	.127	.186	.155	.635	.001	-.073	.112	-.054
Inrole performance 2	.139	.113	.107	.108	.167	.106	.864	.077	.087	.018
Inrole performance 3	.116	.093	.091	.126	.062	.118	.854	.179	.027	.045
Inrole performance 1	.035	.148	.157	.198	.077	.099	.743	.180	.016	.122
Altruism 2	.042	-.067	.042	.035	.022	-.011	.109	.860	.053	.061
Altruism 3	.094	.075	.120	.087	.081	.009	.194	.764	.178	.003
Altruism 1	.001	.154	.130	-.047	.129	.104	.077	.694	.025	.026
Competence2	.096	.134	.054	.087	.121	.082	.092	.062	.892	-.028
Competence1	.149	-.037	.048	.088	.088	.132	.023	.192	.864	.068
Motivational2	.019	.093	-.071	-.038	-.043	-.032	.114	.069	.018	.874
Motivational3	.047	.190	.070	-.044	.084	-.024	.012	.026	.010	.860

Extraction Method: Principal Component Analysis.
Rotation Method: Varimax with Kaiser Normalization.
a. Rotation converged in 6 iterations.

Table 4.3.8.2.5   Reliability Statistics

Cronbach's Alpha	No. of Items
.886	35

The rotated component matrix table shows the loadings of each item on each factor after rotation. The rotated component factor has been grouped as 35 statements into ten factors and on the basis of loading of the statements they are given names and explained below. The cronbach's alpha Reliability statistics found out .886% of the variables reliability.

FACTOR-1 PERSONAL WELLBEING

Following are the major statements loaded in this factor.

* Taking everything together, I'm satisfied in my life as a whole these days.

* I'm satisfied with social life

* I'm satisfied with my family life

* The future looks good for me.

Employees are well aware of their needs at a point. As much as they realize this they should also be aware of the needs, pressures and issues of the people they work with. The learning and knowledge of sharing pose endless possibilities for development, ideas, better communication and understanding between the people. Personal well being is therefore aware of who and what one does, when it has to be done, where it has to be done, how it affects or effects the surroundings. Knowing only pushes boundaries and helps performing better be it with self or rules of the game.

FACTOR-2 CULTURAL INTELLIGENCE

Major statements in this factor are as follows.

* I adjust my cultural knowledge as I interact with people from a culture that is unfamiliar to me.

- I am conscious of the cultural knowledge I apply to cross-cultural interactions.

- I am conscious of the cultural knowledge I use when interacting with people with different cultural backgrounds.

- I check the accuracy of my cultural knowledge as I interact with people from different cultures.

In today's competitive world and culturally diverse society every individual in the organisation must be aware of other culture. Cultural knowledge helps in enhancing communication with their peers and also in serving their customers. In turn it creates a good work environment.

FACTOR-3 SELF-ANXIETY

Following are the major statements loaded in this factor.

- I had to take care of my family

- I had to take care of my health

- I had to be responsible as I am growing old

- I think about how things are going at work

Self-anxiety means amount to which a person reports anxiety about significant importance of their life. In Indian context the focus on family is immense being it a nuclear family or joint family. The working member of the family who is commonly known as the breadwinner looks at multitude of things starting from physiological needs, to safety security, to education and other aspects that form an integral part of family. There is also an increased focus on health. The anxiety around keeping ones health in check is another factor that is deeply rooted in an employee. The fact that there are dependents within the family magnifies the health factor to such an extent that it causes great anxiety.

The need to keep health in check is also one of the factors that causes the needle around self-anxiety fluctuate. The age factor is another self-anxiety trigger. With age comes responsibility and it only increases exponentially. The job in hand therefore becomes very critical. As an employee moves up the age ladder the opportunities become leaner. The factor therefore causes anxiety to hold on, sustain and compromise on the current situation. As with the dole concept nonexistent in India it does force the employee to feel anxious as they grow older. The inclusion of automation as one of the change objectives in any organization and exclusion of human intervention as technology develops and deepens, throws caution to the employee on how things would work in an organization.

FACTOR-4 WORK INVOLVEMENT

Major statements loaded in this factor are as follows

- I am extending my range of abilities.

- I am having enough opportunity to learn new things.

- I am getting enough opportunity to use my abilities.

- I am satisfied with the amount of responsibility given to perform my job.

Employees who feel positive about their jobs can offer you additional brain power, enthusiasm and support. Employee feels engaged when manager operate transparently and keep them abreast of what is happening in the business. As much as possible, let employee knows the company's financial situation, when you land a big contract, and how their work contributes to the success of the business.

FACTOR-5 MOTIVATION

Following are the major statements loaded in this factor.

- I take pride in doing my job as well as I can

- I feel unhappy when my work is not up to my usual standard

- I like to look back on the day's work with a sense of a job well done

- I try to think of ways of doing my job effectively

Employee motivation refers to a temperament to achieve sustained high quality work performance. As such, employee motivation has both task and organisational dimensions. In its task dimension, it designates the willingness to put in discretionary effort, which is likely to be closely related to the perceived interest and usefulness of work tasks. In its organisational dimension, it designates commitment to the employing organisation, which may be reflected in feelings of belongingness, shared values and adequate rewards.

FACTOR-6 JOB SECURITY

Major statements loaded in this factor are as follows.

- There is accountability from my bank to receive salary and other benefits.

- I had steady employment.

- Bank provides stable benefits for me and my family.

A secured job has high degree of influence on better job performance. Perceived job security is likely to explain the importance that individuals attribute to security in their choice of employment. Most individuals plan their future based on the job at hand. So career stability plays an important role in better performance and drives personal happiness. The best way to attain job security is to ensure that one remains as an asset to the employer. This can be done by constantly upgrading skills and widening the field of expertise or taking on challenging projects that others put away because of the risks involved.

FACTOR-7 IN-ROLE PERFORMANCE

Following are the major statements loaded in this factor.

- I fulfill responsibilities specified in job description.

- I am able to perform my tasks that are expected from my manager.

- I will adequately complete assigned duties.

The hustle bustle through which we work often lead to overlooking our purpose in the organisation. Individual performance often results in better organisational performance. It is important that the vision is understood by one and all and how their own contribution towards the goal helps accomplish the mission of an organisation. Doing this, increases involvement, enthusiasm, engagement and improves program delivery. Employee performance reduces ambiguities in the workplace, increases accountability, provides in road for greater performance and ultimately makes one responsible for ones actions or decisions. Employee performance plans therefore must provide for balanced, credible measures.

FACTOR-8 ORGANISATIONAL CITIZENSHIP BEHAVIOR

Major statements loaded in this factor are as follows.

- I am determined to help others who had been absent.

- I am inclined to help who had heavy workloads.

- I am willing to help new employees even though it is NOT required.

Organisational citizenship behavior (OCB) is optional to the employee activity and is not explicitly a part of the job description that tends to promote the organisation. Good behavior only promotes an individual further and influences the organisation to move ahead. So to speak a person displaying good behavior positively influences amongst his/her peers and a person displaying improper behavior influences otherwise. Though the behavior is not a part of the official system and does not hold any rewards or compensation it is often a much talked about topic as to how things may turn for the worse within the team or organisation.

In the recent times it is seen that an individual's behavior has brought an organisation down and an individual's good citizenship behavior has pushed the organisation to greater limits. An employer or employee practicing OCB tends to be more committed to the job than the ones who are not.

FACTOR-9 EMPOWERMENT

Major statements loaded in this factor are as follows.

- I am self-assured about my capabilities to perform my work activities.

- I am confident about my ability to do my job.

Empowerment simply is a faction that will help employee take risk, make decisions with little or no guilt. This however, makes one more accountable and responsible. Employees develop a deep sense of responsibility and pride in the success of the overall program that they are directly involved in, made decisions based on their judgment and feel highly satisfied if the decisions help improve business. This also provides them great opportunity to take on bigger responsibilities and instills immense confidence to do better.

FACTOR-10 PHYSICAL EXPRESSION

Following are the major statements loaded in this factor.

- I change my verbal behavior (e.g., accent, tone) when a cross-cultural interaction requires it.

- I use pause and silence differently to suit different cross-cultural situations.

Cultural intelligence has big influence in the kind of body language displayed. Verbal behavior and punctuations are considered as an important factor in cross-cultural interaction. Knowing the facets of cultures, their body language, their behavior in certain situations etc., will therefore influence the work that one does. Altering ones behavior therefore is of prime importance when interacting with people from different background. This only makes one's job far more interesting and helps others when a situation arises to handle cross-culture person.

4.3.9 TO FIND OUT THE RELATIONSHIP BETWEEN ERM DIMENSIONS AND PW, OC AND OCB.

Employee relationship management gives a clear picture about the employment relations between employees and managers working in leading public sector banks. ERM dimensions are the most influencing factors of employment relations between managers and employees working in public sector banks. For this purpose psychological contract, psychological empowerment, employee involvement, cultural intelligence, psychological ownership, in-role performance, organisational support perceived from their job were considered as dimensions of ERM.

Psychological well-being means satisfaction, happiness, involvement, pleasure of employees and managers derived from their jobs. Organisational commitment means employees and managers believe that they are an integral part of the organisational success and also how emotionally attached they are towards their workplace.

Organisational citizenship behavior is nothing but the employees and managers behavior at their work place. It also has to do with employee participation in management in order to support management function, their hard work, tolerance and maintaining patient, voluntarily helping other employees and also encouraging them to perform their work efficiently when they are actually depressed because of their work.

Multiple regression analysis was conducted to examine the relationship between the ERM dimensions and Psychological well-being, Organisational Commitment and Organisational Citizenship Behavior. For this purpose stepwise regression was adopted further ERM dimensions considered as predictor and PW, OC and OCB as criterion variable.

Hypotheses-11

The ERM dimensions will serve as significant predictors and explain the variance in PW, OC and OCB.

Table 4.3.9 Variables in the Multiple Regression Analysis

Predictor variable	Criterion Variable								
	Psychological well being			Organisational Commitment			Organisational Citizenship behavior		
Employee	B value	T value	P value	B value	T value	P value	B value	T value	P value
(Constant)	73.882	5.711	<0.000	28.511	8.413	<0.000	26.227	3.189	.002**
(x1)	.612	3.021	0.003**	.252	3.852	<0.000	.133	2.669	.008**
(x2)	.281	3.094	0.002**	.488	5.295	<0.000	.539	3.034	.003**
(x3)	.648	2.583	0.010*	.068	2.295	0.023*	.637	2.882	.004**
(x4)	.804	2.331	0.021*	-	-	-	.331	2.122	.035*
(x5)	.240	2.164	0.031*	-	-	-	-	-	-
	$R = .599a$, $R2 = .359$, F = 4.685, p value = 0.031			$R = .579a$, $R2 = .335$, F = 5.266, p value =0.023			$R = .467a$, $R2 = .228$, F =4.501, p value = 0.035		

168 Employee Relationship Management

Table 4.3.9 (Contd.)

Manager	Psychological well being			Organisational Commitment			Organisational Citizenship behavior		
	B value	T value	P value	B value	T value	P value	B value	T value	P value
(Constant)	47.993	2.035	.044*	11.619	1.476	.143	6.337	.457	.649
(x1)	.464	2.960	.004**	.188	3.707	<0.000	.672	2.608	.010*
(x2)	1.336	2.842	.005**	.497	3.691	<0.000	.227	2.427	.017*
(x3)	1.178	2.795	.006**	-	-	-	.275	2.291	.024*

R = .582a, R2 = .339,
F = 7.811, p value = 0.006

R = .540a, R2 = .292,
F = 13.620, p value = < 0.000

R = .548a,
R2 = .301,
F = 5.250,
p value = 0.024

The above table explains the model summary and coefficient of Regression by taking ERM dimensions as a predictor variable to explain its relationship towards the Psychological well-being, Organisational commitment and Organisational citizenship behavior.

4.3.9.1 *Psychological well Being – As a criterion variable*

In Case of Employees

Psychological well-being as a dependent variable - 39.5% of Psychological well-being was explained by the ERM dimensions with the correlation **R = 0.582**, f and p value (**f = 4.685, p value = 0.031**) shows at 5% level of significance there is strong positive relationship between ERM dimensions and Psychological well-being perceived by the public sector bank employee from their job.

ERM dimensions (x) is predictor then dependent variable Psychological well being (y)

$$Y = 73.882 + 0.612x_1 + 0.281x_2 + 0.648x_3 + 0.804x_4 + 0.240x_5$$

Involvement (x_1), Psychological contract (x_2), Psychological Empowerment (x_3), In-role performance (x_4), Cultural Intelligence (x_5).

In Case of Manager

Psychological well-being as a dependent variable – 33.9% of Psychological well-being was explained by the ERM dimensions with the correlation **R = 0.599**, f and p value (**f = 7.811, p value = 0.006**), shows at 1% level of significance there is strong positive relationship between ERM dimensions and Psychological well-being perceived by the public sector bank manager from their job.

ERM dimensions (x) is predictor then dependent variable Psychological well being (y)

$$Y = 47.993 + 0.464x_1 + 1.336x_2 + 1.178x_3$$

Psychological contract (x_1), Organisational support (x_2), Psychological Empowerment (x_3)

Involvement, Psychological contract, Psychological Empowerment, In-Role Performance and Cultural intelligence are considered as an important ERM dimensions that influence the employees Psychological Wellbeing. Psychological Contract, Organisational Support and Psychological Empowerment play a vital role in managers Psychological Wellbeing.

PERCEPTION DIFFERENCE – PSYCHOLOGICAL WELLBEING

Psychological contract and psychological empowerment plays a vital role in perceiving the well-being by both the employee and manager. Further for managers organisational support received from their manager is essential to perceive psychological well-being; whereas it was not in the case of the employee to perceive their well-being. But, involvement, In role performance and cultural intelligence play important role in case of employees to perceive their psychological well-being i.e., satisfaction as a whole It shows that healthy relationship reduces the conflict among employees and also makes them to feel as though they belong to the same family. This is essential for a team work. Team work and inclusive culture can help the organisation to resolve issues. Good relationship between managers/employees helps in building loyalty and trust and thereby driving customer satisfaction. Strong relationship among manager and employee makes them to think positive about their work place.

4.3.9.2   *Organisational commitment – As a criterion variable*

In Case of Employees

Organisational commitment as a dependent variable −33.5% of Organisational commitment was explained by the ERM dimensions with the correlation **R = 0.540** f and p value **f = 5.266, p value =0.023.** It shows that at 5% level of significance there is strong positive relationship between ERM dimensions and commitment towards their work by the public sector bank employees.

ERM dimensions (x) is predictor then dependent variable Organisational commitment (y)

$$Y= 28.551+0.252x_1 + 0.488x_2 +0.068x_3$$

Involvement(x₁), Psychological ownership(x₂), Psychological contract (x₃)

In Case of Manager

Organisational commitment as a dependent variable – 29.2% of Organisational commitment was explained by the ERM dimensions with the correlation **R = .540 f** and p value **f = 13.620, p value =< 0.000.** It shows that at 1% level of significance there is strong positive relationship between ERM dimensions and Organisational commitment towards their work by the public sector bank managers.

ERM dimensions (x) is predictor then dependent variable Organisational Commitment (y)

$$Y= 11.619+0.188x_1+ 0.497x_2$$

Psychological contract (x₁), Psychological Empowerment (x₂)

Involvement, Psychological Ownership and Psychological contract which are considered as an important ERM dimensions influence the employees Organisational Commitment. Psychological Contract and Psychological Empowerment play a vital role in managers Organisational Commitment.

PERCEPTION DIFFERENCE – ORGANIZATIONAL COMMITMENT

Psychological contract is considered as important for both the Employees and Managers committed towards their job. Further psychological empowerment play a vital role in engaging manager towards his/her job, this was not in the employees situation instead, Involvement and their feeling of possession i.e., psychological ownership turns them to be engaged in job. Commitment makes an individual to be engaged and helps them to increase their performance level. An engaged manager is the one who is not only completely immersed and involved with his/her work, it is also how he looks to involve employees who are keen, dedicated and devoted towards their work. An engaged employer works closely with the employee to channelize the organisational objectives in a manner that it is understood. Employer engagement is a willingness to align objectives without much Top Down approach rather an inclusiveness approach. This factor increases better communication between employer and employee and practically dissolves any delineation that may exist.

4.3.9.3   *Organisational Citizenship Behavior– As a criterion variable*

In Case Of Employee

Organisational citizenship behavior as a dependent variable –22.8% of Citizenship behavior of employee was explained by the ERM dimensions with the correlation **R = 0.467** f and p value **F =4.501, p value = 0.035.** It shows that at 5% level of significance there is strong positive relationship between ERM dimensions and Citizenship behavior at their work place by the public sector bank employee.

ERM dimensions (x) is predictor then dependent variable Organisational citizenship behavior (y)

$$Y = 26.227 + 0.133x_1 + 0.539x_2 + 0.637x_3 + 0.331x_4$$

Psychological contract (x_1) Psychological ownership (x_2) In-role performance (x_3) Psychological Empowerment (x_4)

In Case of Manager

Organisational citizenship behavior as a dependent variable – 30.1% of Citizenship behavior of manager was explained by the ERM dimensions with the correlation **R = .548** f and p value **f = 5.250, p value = 0.024.** It shows that at 5% level of significance there is strong positive relationship between ERM dimensions and Organisational Citizenship Behavior of manager working in the public sector banks.

ERM dimensions (x) is predictor then dependent variable Psychological well being (y)

$$Y = 6.337 + 0.672x_1 + 0.227x_2 + 0.275x_3$$

Psychological empowerment (x_1), psychological contract (x_2), Cultural intelligence (x_3)

Psychological Contract, Psychological Ownership, Inrole Performance and Psychological contract which are considered as an important ERM dimensions influence the employees Organisational Citizenship Behavior. Psychological Empowerment, Psychological Contract and Cultural Intelligence play a vital role in managers Organisational Citizenship Behavior.

PERCEPTION DIFFERENCE – ORGANISATIONAL CITIZENSHIP BEHAVIOR

Psychological contract and Empowerment is considered to be an essential factor in determining the citizenship behavior of both employee and manager working in the public sector bank. Further cultural knowledge makes manager to behave at the work place but in case of employees it seems to be not that much essential for their citizenship behavior, on other hand their performance and psychological ownership were considered as an essential factors for their citizenship behavior. Good behavior only promotes that individual further and somewhat influences the organisation to move ahead. So to speak a person displaying good behavior has a good influence amongst his/her peers and a person displaying incorrect behavior influences otherwise. Though the behavior is not a part of the official system and does not hold any rewards or compensation it is often a much-talked topic as to how things may turn for the worse within the team or organisation. An employer or employee practicing OCB tends to be more committed to the job than the ones who are not. Some of the attributes that an OCB include are sportsmanship, continued involvement in professional and social environment and the open arm acceptance of rules and regulations of an organisation.

4.3.10 DISCRIMINANT ANALYSIS

Discriminant analysis was used to find how much percentage of sample data was correctly classified. Further this analysis also helps predict outcomes by providing discriminant functions that act as regression equations.

Table 4.3.10.1 Group Statistics

ERM Dimensions	Manager	Employee	Total	Wilks' Lambda	F value	P value
Psychological contract	151.89 (13.737)	139.27 (18.325)	143.25 (17.979)	.893	43.283	<0.000
Psychological Empowerment	49.23 (5.163)	46.12 (5.674)	47.10 (5.698)	.936	25.026	<0.000
Involvement	48.70 (7.772)	45.67 (8.318)	46.63 (8.261)	.971	10.902	0.001**

ERM Dimensions	Manager	Employee	Total	Wilks' Lambda	F value	P value
Cultural Intelligence	73.50 (11.323)	69.48 (12.553)	70.75 (12.306)	.977	8.544	0.004**
Psychological ownership	30.16 (4.755)	27.66 (4.869)	28.44 (4.965)	.945	21.083	<0.000
Organisational support	29.31 (4.566)	27.49 (5.049)	28.06 (4.968)	.971	10.917	0.001**
In role performance	27.20 (3.277)	25.73 (3.738)	26.19 (3.659)	.965	13.171	<0.000
Psychological wellbeing	215.53 (24.611)	208.24 (23.944)	210.53 (24.360)	.981	7.183	0.008**
Organisational Commitment	64.61 (7.989)	62.93 (7.873)	63.46 (7.937)	.990	3.539	0.061
Organisational citizenship behavior	94.13 (14.095)	91.31 (13.842)	92.20 (13.964)	.991	3.237	0.073

** Denotes significant at 1% level. 2. * Denotes significant at 5% level

This table provides the descriptive statistics (mean (SD)) for the two categorized by ERM dimensions (Psychological contract, psychological empowerment, employee involvement, cultural intelligence, psychological ownership, organisational support and in role performance) and also PW, OC and OCB. The table 4.3.10.1 was generated by the selected Univariate ANOVAs. The results indicate that there is a statistical significant difference among the psychological wellbeing for each dimensions of ERM. Whereas, organisational commitment and organisational citizenship behavior is insignificant towards ERM dimensions.

BOX'S TEST OF EQUALITY OF COVARIANCE MATRICES

Box's M tests the assumption of multivariate homogeneity of covariance, i.e., it determines whether the covariance matrices for the groups are equivalent.

Table 4.3.10.2   Log Determinants

Designation	Rank	Log Determinant
Manager	10	38.057
Employees	10	39.680
Pooled within-groups	10	39.426

The ranks and natural logarithms of determinants printed are those of the group covariance matrices.

Table 4.3.10.3   Test Results

Box's M		92.776
F	Approx	1.628
	df1	55
	df2	174377.780
	Sig.	.002

Tests null hypothesis of equal population covariance matrices.

The ranks and natural logarithms of determinants printed are those of the group covariance matrices.

The first table under Box's Test of Equality of Covariance Matrices is the Log Determinants table. It provides the natural log of the determinants of each group's covariance matrix and a log determinant for the covariance matrix that would result if the two groups were combined, i.e., the pooled within-groups measure (note: the 'rank' number is simply the number of Designation). Since Discriminant analysis assumes homogeneity of covariance matrices between groups, the group determinants ideally should be nearly equal to one another.

Table 4.3.10.4   Summary of Canonical Discriminant Functions

Function	Eigenvalue	% of Variance	Cumulative %	Wilks' Lambda	P value	Canonical Correlation
1	.176(a)	100.0	100.0	.851	.000	.387

A First 1 canonical discriminant functions were used in the analysis.

The above table explains the eigenvalues and canonical correlations for the computed discriminant functions. An eigenvalue indicates the proportion of variance explained. (Between-groups sums of squares divided by within-groups sums of squares). A large eigenvalue is associated with a strong function. The canonical relation is a correlation between the discriminant scores and the levels of the dependent variable. A high correlation indicates a function that discriminates well. Even though the eigenvalue is less but the canonical correlation moderately relates to the ERM dimensions with a value of 0.387.

The table 4.3.10.4 shows the Wilks' Lambda is the ratio of within-groups sums of squares to the total sums of squares. This is the proportion of the total variance in the discriminant scores not explained by differences among groups. Here, the Lambda of 0.851 has a significant value (Sig. = < 0.000) and the associated significance value indicates the difference is significant. Therefore, the group means (Mean of managers and employees) appear to differ.

Thus, in discriminant analysis, an eigenvalue represents the relative amount of variance that the linear combination ERM dimensions and also PW, OC and OCB within the managers and employees working in the public sector banks. Therefore canonical correlation proves that there is a positive relationship between ERM dimensions individual wellbeing dimensions and OCB among employees and managers.

Table 4.3.10.5 Canonical Discriminant Function Coefficients

	Function 1
Psychological contract	.047
Psychological Empowerment	.073
Psychological ownership	-.016
In role performance	-.005
Organisational support	.083
Involvement	-.023
Cultural Intelligence	.066
Psychological wellbeing	-.005

	Function 1
Commitment	-.037
Organisational citizenship behavior	-.005
(Constant)	-8.627
Unstandardized coefficients	

The 'Canonical Discriminant Function Coefficients' indicate the unstandardized scores concerning the independent variables. It is the list of coefficients of the unstandardized discriminant equation. Each dimensions discriminant score would be computed by entering his or her variable values (raw data) for each of the variables in the equation. Unstandardized discriminant function coefficients for each computed function.

These are equivalent to the unstandardized b (regression) coefficients in multiple regression i.e., it is used to construct the equation that computes the discriminant score for that function for each subject in the analysis.

This formula is constructed as follows (where D = the discriminant score for a subject; a = the function constant; b = the unstandardized coefficients for each independent variable (X); and n = the number of independent variables)

$$D = a + b_1 X_1 + b_2 X_2 + \dots b_n X_n$$

$$D = -8.627 + 0.047_{x1} + 0.073_{x2} - 0.016_{x3} - 0.005_{x4} + 0.083_{x5} - 0.023_{x6} + 0.066_{x7} - 0.005_{x8} - 0.037_{x9} - 0.005_{x10}$$

Psychological contract (x_1), Psychological Empowerment (x_2), Psychological ownership (x_3), In-role performance (x_4), Organisational support (x_5), Involvement (x_6), Cultural Intelligence (x_7), Psychological wellbeing (x_8), Organisational commitment (x_9), Organisational citizenship behavior (x_{10}).

Table 4.3.10.6   Functions at Group Centroids

Designation	Function
	1
Manager	.616
Employees	-.284

Unstandardized canonical discriminant functions evaluated at group means

The above Group Centroids table shows the mean value of the two groups' (Managers and employees) discriminant scores, computed using the discriminant function equation previously described. Discriminant analysis will compute one group centroids for each category or group defined by the dependent variable for each discriminant function.

More specifically, the discriminant score for each group when the variable means (rather than individual values for each subject) are entered into the discriminant equation. Note that the two scores are equal in absolute value but have opposite signs.

The value of Discriminant function (D) is -.284, which shows that person who attains this value or close to this value belongs to employee grade and those who attain the 0.616 or above belong to manager.

Table 4.3.10.7   Classification Results (A)

		Designation	Predicted Group Membership		Total
			Manager	Employees	
Original	Count	Manager	83	32	115
		Employees	75	175	250
	%	Manager	72.2	27.8	100.0
		Employees	30.0	70.0	100.0

The above classification table provides results of the success rate for prediction of membership through grouping variable's categories and also based on the coefficients of their predictor variables developed from the analysis. Employees were more accurately classified with

70% of the cases correct and in the case of Managers it is 72.2% of cases were correctly classified. Overall, 70.7% of the original cases were correctly classified.

The classification (30%) might be due to that employees think similarly as a manager because they may be experienced and waiting for their promotions. Likewise, 27.8% of managers similarly think like an employee because they may be newly promoted from employee grade.

4.3.11 TO PROPOSE A MODEL TOWARDS THE RELATION-SHIP BETWEEN ERM DIMENSIONS AND PSYCHOLOGICAL WELL-BEING, ORGANISATIONAL COMMITMENT AND ORGANISATIONAL CITIZENSHIP BEHAVIOR.

Hypotheses 12

The ERM dimensions will have a positive significant relationship with PW, OC and OCB.

A model is a theory which explains the relationship among different variables. The model is essentially a statistical statement about the relationship among the variables (Hoyle 1995). In order to understand the relationship among the variables under investigation the author has proposed model, explaining about the relationship among the ERM dimensions, individual well being variable and work place behavior based on the previous studies of Rousseau's (2008), Spreitzer, Gretchen M. (1996), Allen & Mayer (1991), Eisternberg's (1986), Williams & Anderson (1991), Podsakoff and MacKenzie (1997), Linn Van Dyne (2004),(2006), Lawler (1988) and Warr & cook (1979).

A few alternative models were tried and this model offered best theoretical and empirical fit. AMOS software is used to develop this model. In AMOS graphics, the observed variables are represented with rectangles and linear equation are represented with arrows from the IV to the DV. AMOS graphics also represents the results from analysis in a visual framework that is very easy to understand. The initial step in model development is a specification of model as a path diagram and model must include a residual error term (e) as an ellipse which indicate latent or immeasurable variable. The path diagram specification of the model also highlights that the predictor variables are co-related in the model.

To perform the AMOS analysis and also to find a mediatory relationship between dependent and independent variable, the predicator variables are entered in set of variables according to predetermined order that may infer some casual or potentially mediating relationship between predictors and the dependent variable (Meyer et al, 2006).

THE VARIABLES USED IN THE STRUCTURAL EQUATION MODEL ARE

1. OBSERVED, ENDOGENOUS VARIABLES

    1. Psychological Well-being

    2. Organizational Commitment

    3. Organizational Citizenship Behavior

2. OBSERVED, EXOGENOUS VARIABLES

    1. Psychological Contract

    2. Psychological Empowerment

    3. Employee Involvement

    4. Psychological Ownership

    5. Organizational Support

    6. In-Role Performance

    7. Cultural Intelligence

3. UNOBSERVED, EXOGENOUS VARIABLES

    1. e1: Error term for Psychological contract.

    2. e2: Error term for Psychological Empowerment.

    3. e3: Error term for Employee Involvement.

4. e4: Error term for Cultural Intelligence.

5. e5: Error term for Psychological Ownership.

6. e6: Error term for Organizational Support.

7. e7: Error term for In-role performance.

8. e8: Error term for Psychological Well-being.

9. e9: Error term for Organizational Commitment.

10. e10: Error term for Organizational Citizenship Behavior.

HENCE NUMBERS OF VARIABLE IN THE SEM ARE

Number of variables in your model:	21
Number of observed variables:	10
Number of unobserved variables:	11
Number of exogenous variables:	11
Number of endogenous variables:	3

Table 4.3.11.1   Variables in the Structural Equation Model Analysis

			Unstandardized Regression Weights	S.E.	Standardized Regression Weights	P
PW	<---	ERM	16.097	1.206	13.345	***
OC	<---	ERM	4.753	.403	11.792	***
OCB	<---	PW	.148	.023	6.487	***
OCB	<---	OC	1.003	.070	14.314	***
CI	<---	ERM	6.838	.637	10.741	***
PO	<---	ERM	2.766	.258	10.710	***
OS	<---	ERM	3.348	.249	13.436	***
RP	<---	ERM	1.734	.197	8.817	***
INV	<---	ERM	6.101	.400	15.239	***
PE	<---	ERM	3.605	.286	12.627	***
PC	<---	ERM	13.604	.851	15.983	***

Note: ***denotes significant at 1% level

Here the coefficient of **ERM** is 16.097 and it represents the partial effect of ERM towards PW dimensions on employees and managers working in public sector bank. The estimated positive sign implies that such effect is positive that PW would increase by 16.097 for every unit increase in perception towards ERM and this coefficient value is significant at 1% level.

The coefficient of **ERM** towards OC is 4.753 and it represents the partial effect of awareness towards Commitment of employee and managers working in the public sector bank. The estimated positive sign implies that such effect is positive that OC would increase by 4.753 for every unit increase in perception towards ERM and this coefficient value is significant at 1% level.

The coefficient of **PW** is 0.148 and it represents the partial effect of attitude towards citizenship behavior of both employee and manager as constant. The estimated positive sign implies that such effect is positive that PW would increase by 0.148 for every unit increase in attitude towards citizenship behavior and this coefficient value is significant at 1% level.

Figure 4.3.11   Model for ERM Dimensions, Individual Wellbeing and Work Place Behavior Variables.

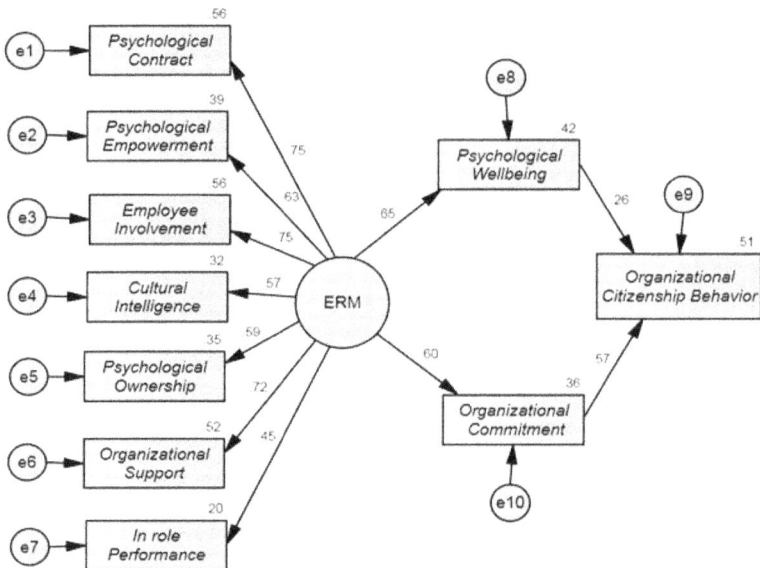

The coefficient of **ERM** towards CI is 6.838 and it represents the partial effect of ERM towards CI, further ERM holding PO, OS, RP, INV, PE and PC with the values of 2.766, 3.348, 1.734, 6.101, 3.605, 13.604. The estimated positive sign implies that such effect is positive that CI, PO, OS, RP, INV, PE and PC would increase by 6.838, 2.766, 3.348, 1.734, 6.101, 3.605, and 13.604 for every unit increase in attitude towards CI, PO, OS, RP, INV, PE and PC and this coefficient value is significant at 1% level.

Table 4.3.11.2   Fit Measures of the Model

Chi-square value	GFI	AGFI	CFI	NFI	RMR	ECVI	RMSEA
67.467	0.964	0.942	0.975	0.951	0.000	0.301	0.052

The fitness measures of the model (4.3.11.2.) shows that the GF1 and CFI value is 0.96, 0.975 indicating a perfect model fit and the AGF1 value (0.94) is also closer to one indicating acceptable model fit. The RMSEA value is smaller (.05) indicating better model. Expected cross validation index (ECVI) is an estimate of how well one can apply the result obtained from one sample that can be generalized to another sample. The values generated always remain positive and closer to zero. The value of ECVI in this model is 0.30 indicating the model can be generalized for other samples. Further relationships between these variables are as follows.

1. Psychological contract and employee involvement has strong positive relationship towards ERM with the correlation of 0.75.

2. Organizational support towards ERM with the correlation of 0.72.

3. Psychological empowerment towards ERM with the correlation of 0.63.

4. Psychological ownership towards ERM with the correlation of 0.59.

5. Cultural intelligence towards ERM with the correlation of 0.57.

6. In-role performance towards ERM with the correlation of 0.45.

7. Relationship of ERM towards the dimensions of individual wellbeing i.e., towards psychological wellbeing with the value of 0.65 and towards organizational commitment with the value of 0.60

8. Psychological wellbeing towards organizational citizenship behavior with the value of 0.26 shows that there is poor relationship and organizational commitment towards organizational citizenship behavior with the value of 0.57 which is closer 0.6 shows that there is a positive relationship between organizational commitment and citizenship behavior.

The model (fig. 4.3.11.) clearly explains relationship between psychological contract, psychological empowerment, employee involvement, cultural intelligence, psychological ownership, organisational support, in-role performance towards ERM and ERM towards individual wellbeing and work place behavior. This may be because of employees and managers working in the public sector banks might give more importance to loyalty, which leads to trust, support each other, in turn improve the performance. Once the employees receive support from their managers they easily get involved in the work, also it empowers and make them to feel the possession of ownership about the bank. Over the period of time this behavior eradicate the cross-culture negative thought. Instead, employees may begin to practice the other culture and also handle the cross-cultural situations.

Further model explains that there exists a positive and significant relationship among the ERM dimensions towards individual well being and OCB. Hence, the hypothesis is accepted.

5

FINDINGS AND CONCLUSIONS

5.1 INTRODUCTION

Research has to provide clarity in the results and this is achieved through adequate measurement of the variables under study and accurate inferences from the result of analysis. Empirical research helps in establishing meaningful and logical relationship among the variables. This chapter discusses outcome of the author's analysis on ERM and its implication on the organisational settings.

5.2 SUMMARY OF FINDINGS

1. In case of Managers - 83.5% respondents of the study conducted by the author belonged to male and 16.5% female. Therefore more male respondents were in the manager grade and more female respondents were in the employee grade.

    In case of Employees - 47% respondents of the study belonged to male category and 53% respondents of them belonged to female category.

2. In case of Managers - 93% respondents of this study were married and 7% respondents were unmarried.

    In case of Employees - 79.2% of respondents of this study were married and 20.8% respondents were unmarried.

3. In case of Managers - 60% respondents were graduates, 33.9% respondents were post-graduates and 6.1% respondents belonged to other category like ITI, C.A (IIB) and B.Tech. Hence maximum respondents were at least graduates.

    In case of Employees- 57.6% respondents were graduates, 35.2% respondents were post-graduates and 7.2% respondents belonged to other category. Other categories include ITI, C.A (IIB), B.Tech.

4. In case of Managers - 13.9% respondents were earning between 3-5lakhs, 38.3% respondents were earning between 5-7lakhs and 47.8% respondents were earning above 7lakhs.

    In case of Employees - 32.8% respondents were earning up to Rs 3lakhs p.a., 34% respondents were earning between 3-5 lakhs, 30.4% respondents were earning between 5-7lakhs, 2.8% respondents earning above 7 lakhs.

5. In case of Managers - 4.3% respondents belonged to below 30 yrs of age, 13% respondents belonged to 31-40 yrs of age, 17.4% respondents belonged to 41-50 yrs of age and 65.2% respondents belonged to above 50 yrs age. Therefore maximum numbers of respondents are more than 50 years of age.

    In case of Employees - 32% respondents belonged to up to 30 years of age, 14.8% respondents belonged to 31-40 yrs of age, 22% respondents belonged to 41-50 yrs of age and 31.2% respondents belonged to above 50 yrs age.

6. In case of Managers - 7% respondents were having up to 10yrs of experience, 13% respondents were having between 11-20yrs of experience, 30.4% respondents were having between 21-30yrs of experience, and 49.6% respondents were having above 31 years of experience.

    In case of Employees - 34.4% respondents were having up to 10yrs of experience, 17.2% respondents were having between 11-20yrs of experience, 27.2% respondents were having between 21-30yrs of experience and 21.2% respondents were having above 31 years of experience.

7. More than 90% of both employees and managers feel that they need friends at their work place.

8. More than 90% of both employees and managers feel that socialising at work place is very much important to achieve their task easily.

9. 90% of managers think that networking is very much essential to expand their business, but only 74% of employees feel that they need networking with larger organisation.

10. 55% of managers discuss their personal issues with his/her friend; almost 63% of employees discuss their personal issue with their friends, which in turn help them to find solution.

11. 90% of employees and managers working in the public sector banks feel happy about the current employment. It seems that their obligations were met by each other.

12. 96% of managers were satisfied with the growth opportunity in their job whereas only 82% of employees were satisfied with the growth opportunity.

13. 85% of managers working in the public sector banks accepted that they were living comfortable life whereas only 75% of employees working in the public sector banks feel that they lead a comfortable life.

14. Almost 94% of both employees and managers working in the public sector bank accepted that they were receiving appropriate training from the organisation to perform their duties efficiently.

15. 85% of managers working in the public sector banks do not have an idea to quit their job; likewise 76% of employees are not planning to quit their job. This shows that they were very much satisfied with their job.

16. Nearly 30% of managers often thought about their job even though they were not actually at work, but almost 43% of employees sometimes think about their work even though they were out of the work.

17. More than 63% of managers as well as employees feel happy in spending their time at work.

18. Nearly 40% of both the employees and managers working in the public sector banks sometimes feel depressed because of their extensive work pressure. Approximately 10% of both the managers and employees feel often depressed in their work place.

19. To find whether sample population represents the total population, Normality test was performed. Since p value in all ERM dimension and also PW, OC and OCB is greater than 0.05 therefore

null hypotheses is accepted. Hence the sample population (Employee $_{n1}$= 250, Managers $_{n2}$ = 115) represents the opinion of the total population.

20. To find out the reliability of the collected data reliability analysis was performed. Cronbach's Alpha is greater than 0.50 in all dimensions and sub dimension of ERM, PW, OC and OCB, further for over all dimensions it is 0.966 i.e., 96.6% of data were reliable. Therefore it is statistically proved that the data collected for the study is more reliable and considered for further analysis.

21. To identify the differences between employee and manager with regards to ERM dimensions and Psychological Well-Being, Organisational Commitment and Organisational Citizenship Behavior, independent t test was performed. The P value is less than 0.01, in all dimensions of ERM, the null hypothesis is rejected at 1% level of significance. Hence it is concluded that there is significant difference between employee and managers working in the public sector bank towards the perception of ERM. Manager's level of perception towards ERM is quite better than employee's perception towards ERM.

22. To find out the difference of option about psychological contract between manager and employee and also to find the relationship between employees and manager working in the public sector bank, independent t test was performed. Except in case of erosion, other dimensions of psychological contract is statistically proved at 1% level that there is a significant difference between perception of employees and managers working in public sector banks.

23. To find out the perception differences about psychological empowerment among manager and employee and also to find the relationship between employees and managers working in the public sector bank through their psychological empowerment, independent t test was performed.

   Except in case of competence other dimensions of psychological empowerment is statistically proved at 1% level that there is a significant difference between perception of employees and managers working in public sector banks.

24. To determine the significant differences between managers and employees perception towards their Involvement independent t test was used. It is statistically proved at 5% level that there is a significant difference between perception of employees and managers working in public sector banks towards employee involvement dimensions.

25. To find the perception differences regarding cultural intelligence among managers and employees working in the public sector bank and also to find the relationship between them through their cultural knowledge, independent t test was performed. Except in case of metacognitive and behavioral, other dimensions of cultural intelligence is statistically proved at 5% level that there is a significant difference between perception of employees and managers working in public sector banks towards ERM.

26. To analyze the perception differences about other dimensions of ERM such as perceived organisational support, psychological ownership and in-role performance among managers and employees, independent t test was carried out. It is statistically proved at 1% level that there is a significant difference between perception of employees and managers working in public sector banks towards psychological ownership, perceived organisational support and in-role performance.

27. To identify the differences between employees and managers with regard to psychological well-being, organisational commitment and organisational citizenship behavior, independent t test was carried out. Psychological wellbeing is statistically proved at 1% level that there is a significant difference between employees and managers working in public sector banks. But in case of commitment and citizenship behaviors even at 5% level both were insignificant.

28. To analyze the perception differences about psychological well-being among manager and employee and also to understand the relationship between employees and manager working in the public sector bank through their well-being, Independent t test was carried out. Except in case of work involvement, intrinsic job motivation, life satisfaction, happiness and self anxiety, other dimensions

of psychological wellbeing were statistically proved at 1% level that there is a significant difference between perception of employees and managers working in public sector banks.

29. To determine the significant differences between managers and employees perception towards their commitment, independent t test was performed. Except in case of continuance and normative commitment other dimension of commitment i.e., affective commitment is statistically proved at 1% level that there is significant difference between employees and managers working in public sector banks.

30. To find out the employees and managers difference towards their citizenship behavior in the bank, independent t test was carried out. Except in case of altruism and sportsmanship, other dimensions of organizational citizenship behavior is statistically proved at 5% level that there is no significant difference between employees and managers working in public sector banks.

31. To know the significant difference between income level of employees and managers towards ERM dimensions, individual well-being dimensions, work place behavior ANOVA was performed. The test result indicates that at 5% level of significant, employees organisational support was influenced by their income level.

32. To know the significant difference between age group of employees and managers towards ERM dimensions, individual well-being dimensions, work place behavior ANOVA was performed. The test result of ANOVA indicates that there is no significant difference between age group of employees and managers towards certain ERM dimensions, individual well-being dimensions and their work place behavior. The findings also explain that involvement and performance of managers were influenced by their age.

33. To know the significant difference between educational background of employees and managers towards ERM dimensions, individual well-being dimensions and work place behavior ANOVA was performed. The ANOVA results explain that there is no significant difference between employees and managers level of education with regards to psychological contract, psychological empowerment, employee involvement, cultural intelligence, psy-

chological ownership, organisational support and psychological wellbeing. Whereas, in case of managers in-role performance, organisational commitment and organisational citizenship behavior was influenced by levels of education.

34. To know the significant difference between gender composition of employees and managers towards ERM dimensions, individual well-being dimensions, and work place behavior t test was performed. The result shows even at 5% level that there is no significant difference between employees and managers gender composition with respect to certain ERM dimension, psychological wellbeing and organisational citizenship behavior. As far as the gender composition of the ERM is concerned, both male and female individuals in the bank are having more or less the same perception about psychological contract, psychological empowerment, employee involvement, cultural intelligence, psychological ownership, perceived organisational support, psychological wellbeing and organisational citizenship behavior. Whereas, at 5% level there is a significant differences between employees in-role performance and managers organisational commitment.

35. To know the significant difference between marital status of employees and managers towards ERM dimensions, individual well-being dimensions, and work place behavior t test was performed. The result indicates that there is no significant difference between employee's marital status on ERM dimensions, psychological wellbeing, organisational commitment and organisational citizenship behavior. In case of managers there is a significant difference between marital status on cultural intelligence, organisational commitment and organisational citizenship behavior. The mean score of married and unmarried employees are similar; therefore, there is no significant difference between ERM dimensions, individual well-being dimensions, organisational citizenship behavior and marital status. But in case of managers cultural intelligence, organisational commitment and organisational citizenship behavior the mean score of unmarried is higher than married managers.

36. To know the significant difference between educational background of employees and managers towards ERM dimensions, individual well-being dimensions and work place behavior ANOVA

was performed. The findings of the one way ANOVA explain even at 5% level that there is no significant difference between work experience of employees and managers towards ERM dimensions, PW, OC and OCB. The mean score of variables were similar and it shows that employees and managers perceptions towards these variables are not influenced by their work experience.

37. To find out the association between job Satisfaction and happiness perceived from the work, chi-square analysis was performed. Phi and Cramer's V tests the strength of association. It shows that the strength of association between the variables is very strong. The asymptotic significance of employees in the test statistics is 0.000 and is 0.001 for managers which are less than 0.05. Hence null hypothesis is rejected and research hypothesis is accepted; therefore there is a significant association between "Happiness and Job satisfaction". It is concluded that there is a strong positive association between the "Happiness and Job satisfaction of the employees and managers working in the public sector bank".

38. To know the statistical association between friendly relationship and age level of managers working in public sector banks ANOVA was performed. The output of the ANOVA explains that p value in case of employees is 0.096 which is more than 5% level, therefore, null hypotheses is accepted. There is no statistical significant difference in friendly relationship and age level of employees working in public sector banks. Whereas, p value in case of managers is 0.023 which is less than 5% level, therefore, research hypotheses was accepted. There is a statisticaly significant difference between friendly relationship and age level of managers working in public sector banks.

39. To know the influencing dimensions of ERM for both employees and managers factor analysis was performed. In case of manager the KMO value is 0.772 it shows the sample adequacy, with the variance (71.772%) and reliability (0.949). In case of employees the KMO value is 0.803 with the variance (71.890%) and reliability (0.886). Psychological wellbeing, work involvement, organisational citizenship behavior, cultural intelligence were the four main factors influencing ERM of managers and employees working in public sector banks.

40. To find out the relationship between ERM dimensions and psychological wellbeing, multiple regression was performed. The result is as follows.

    In case of employees: Involvement, psychological contract, psychological empowerment, in-role performance and cultural intelligence represent ERM and it has significant influence over psychological well-being.

    In case of Manager: Psychological contract, organisational support and psychological empowerment, cultural intelligence represent ERM and it has significant influence over psychological well-being.

41. To find out the relationship between ERM dimensions and organisational commitment, multiple regression was performed. The result is as follows.

    In case of employees: Involvement, psychological ownership and psychological contract represent the ERM and it has significant influence over organisational commitment.

    In case of Manager: Psychological contract and psychological empowerment represent the ERM and it has significant influence over organisational commitment.

42. To find out the relationship between ERM dimensions and organisational citizenship behavior, multiple regression was performed. The result is as follows.

    In case of Employee: Psychological contract, psychological ownership, in-role performance and psychological empowerment represent the ERM and it has significant influence over organisational citizenship behavior.

    In case of Manager: Psychological empowerment, psychological contract and cultural intelligence represent the ERM and it has significant influence over organisational citizenship behavior.

43. To know the correct classification of data, discriminant analysis was performed. Discriminant classification table provides results of the success rate for prediction of membership through cat-

egories of grouping variables and also based on the coefficients of their predictor variables developed from the analysis. 70% of the cases (Employees) were classified correctly and 72.2% of cases (Managers) were correctly classified. Overall, 70.7% of the original cases were correctly classified.

44. To propose a model towards the relationship between ERM Dimensions and Psychological Well-Being, Organisational Commitment and Organisational Citizenship Behavior, Structural equation modeling was performed. Model fit summary GF1 and CFI value is 0.96, 0.975 indicating a perfect model fit and the AGF1 value (0.94) is also closer to one indicating acceptable model fit. The RMSEA value is smaller (.05) indicating better model. Expected cross validation index (ECVI) is an estimate of how well one can apply the result obtained from one sample that can be generalized to another sample. The values generated always remain positive and closer to zero. The value of ECVI in this model is 0.30 indicating the model can be generalized for other samples.

5.3 SUGGESTIONS

Employer–employee should maintain a cordial relation. Inter-personal relationship and mutual belief should be always there which helps to maintain a good understanding between the employer and employees. Likewise mutual trust is revered and employees need to treat each other with due respect to avoid relationship problems. The relationship between managers and employees is bitter in some situation. It might be because of work pressure of employees or adverse attitudes showed by their manager. Therefore, author's study provides some suggestion for the manager, employees and management for improved relations.

5.3.1 To Employees

1. Friendliness will help to improve a healthy relationship with others during all the situations. Both the employee as well as manager in every branch should work hand in hand for the development of the organisation.

2. Employees should be loyal towards their manager in order to create the peaceful work atmosphere. This helps to build a strong

mutual trust in their manager and leads to gain positive work support. Understanding the expectations of their manager helps every employee to fulfil his/her obligation, further it improves the self responsibilities towards their work.

3. A lot of youngsters got into banking sector; they must be punctual, compliment each others, respect elders and also need to be a good listener. Involving employees in making work related decisions, obtaining their suggestions motivates them to perform their work actively.

4. Maintaining warmth and sense of belongingness in order to install Together Everyone Achieves More – TEAM which may lead to bilateral discussions, de-liberalization and interaction and helps employees to be self motivated which is useful for their future career development.

5. An employee should try to have his/her identity with employer. Interest in employer growth which in turn helps employee's growth and personal touch is a must to understand each other in a better way (personal interaction / frequent meetings, get together to have a friendly relationship).

5.3.2 To Manager

1. Managers should feel the self-satisfaction in their assignments. Regulated working hours and frequent team meetings will increase bonding among employees.

2. Managers should believe their employees, which in turn will improve the trust within the organisation.

3. There should be an open discussion between managers – employees to know the recent issues in their bank.

4. Suitable reward/punishment system for performing/sulking employee should be introduced. Human values has to be given more importance. PSU Bank employee's average age is more and need VRS. In such cases new employees should be recruited so that there is time for relationship.

5.3.3   To Management

1. HR principles that remain in paper are to be implemented.

2. Employer–Employee relationship is not a master slave relationship. Moreover in PSBs, employees are recruited after tough exams and are really capable.

3. The management shall utilize the talents of every employee and manager by recognizing their work and giving scope for them to come out with their potentials.

4. Regular and proper communication is needed at all levels. An initiative from the management will resolve the issues.

5. Empathy, concerns, recognition and appreciations are required for every project/ achievements.

6. There is a lot of scope for improving manager–employee relationship by conducting seminars, workshops to understand the requirements of manager and expectations of the employees.

5.4   CONCLUSION

A relationship is healthy only if expectations are set in a manner that is fair and realistic. For a healthy relationship between Employer/ Employee the same holds good. In the study conducted by the author, it seems that if a manager and employee are able to satisfy each other's obligations it will build a better working environment and thereby improve relationship. Every employee in an organisation spends maximum time at their work place; therefore it is more than imperative to treat them as a part of extended family. A small initiative that is more associated to fun and celebration can go a long way in building better employee engagement that results in better commitment. Strong employment relation helps employees to maintain good work culture and good work environment. Culture makes the employees emotionally attached towards the organisation. Technical knowledge is required in order to improve the relationship between the youngsters and experienced employee.

END NOTES

1. Shore, L. M., & Tetrick, L. E. (1994). The psychological contract as an explanatory framework in the employment relationship. *Trends in organizational behavior, 1*(91), 107.http://psycnet.apa.org/psycinfo/1994-98115-007

2. Roehling, M., Cavanaugh, M. A., Moynihan, L., & Boswell, W. R. (1998). The nature of the new employment relationship (s): A content analysis of the practitioner and academic literatures. *Center for Advanced Human Resource Studies CAHRS Working Paper Series*. Paper 130. http://digitalcommons.ilr.cornell.edu/cahrswp/130.

3. Millward, L. J., & Brewerton, P. M. (1999). Contractors and their psychological contracts. *British Journal of Management*, *10*(3), 253-274.

4. Coyle Shapiro, J., & Kessler, I. (2000). Consequences of the psychological contract for the employment relationship: A large scale survey. *Journal of management studies*, *37*(7), 903-930.

5. Guest, D. E., & Conway, N. (2002). Communicating the psychological contract: An employer perspective. *Human Resource Management Journal*, *12*(2), 22-38.

6. Coyle Shapiro, J. A. M. (2002). A psychological contract perspective on organizational citizenship behavior. *Journal of Organizational Behavior*, *23*(8), 927-946.

7. Conway, N., & Briner, R. B. (2002). Full-time versus part-time employees: Understanding the links between work status, the psychological contract, and attitudes. *Journal of Vocational Behavior, 61*(2), 279-301. doi:10.1006/jvbe.2001.1857

8.   Coyle-Shapiro, J. A. M., & Kessler, I. (2002). Exploring reciprocity through the lens of the psychological contract: Employee and employer perspectives. *European journal of work and organizational psychology, 11*(1), 69-86. http://eprints.Ise.ac.uk/archive/00000833.

9.   LS. Lambert, Edwards J.R. & Cable, D.M. (2003). Breach and Fulfillment of the Psychological Contract: A Comparison of Traditional and Expanded Views. *Personnel Psychology, 56*(4), 895-934. http://onlinelibrary.wiley.com/doi/10.1111/j.1744-6570.2003.tb00244.x/pdf

10.   Dabos, G. E., & Rousseau, D. M. (2004). Mutuality and reciprocity in the psychological contracts of employees and employers. *Journal of Applied Psychology, 89*(1), 52.

11.   Kickul, J., Lester, S. W., & Belgio, E. (2004). Attitudinal and Behavioral Outcomes of Psychological Contract Breach A Cross Cultural Comparison of the United States and Hong Kong Chinese. *International Journal of Cross Cultural Management, 4*(2), 229-252. doi: 10.1177/1470595804044751

12.   Sutton, G., & Griffin, M. A. (2004). Integrating expectations, experiences, and psychological contract violations: A longitudinal study of new professionals. *Journal of Occupational and Organizational Psychology, 77*(4), 493-514.

13.   Coyle-Shapiro, J. A., & Conway, N. (2005). Exchange relationships: examining psychological contracts and perceived organizational support. *Journal of applied psychology, 90*(4), 774. http://eprints.Ise.ac.uk/archive/00000828.

14.   Coyle Shapiro, J. A. M., Morrow, P. C., & Kessler, I. (2006). Serving two organizations: exploring the employment relationship of contracted employees. *Human Resource Management, 45*(4), 561-583. http://eprints.Ise.ac.uk/archive/2655

15.   Coyle-Shapiro, J. A., & Shore, L. M. (2007). The employee–organization relationship: Where do we go from here?. *Human Resource Management Review*, 17(2), 166-179. DOI: 10.1016/j.hrmr.2007.03.008

16. Spreitzer, G. M. (1996). Social structural characteristics of psychological empowerment. *Academy of Management Journal,* 39(2), 483-504.

17. Spreitzer, G. M., Kizilos, M. A., & Nason, S. W. (1997). A dimensional analysis of the relationship between psychological empowerment and effectiveness satisfaction, and strain. *Journal of management, 23*(5), 679-704.

18. Kirkman, B. L., & Rosen, B. (1999). Beyond self-management: Antecedents and consequences of team empowerment. *Academy of Management Journal, 42*(1), 58-74. http://www.jstor.org/page/info/about/policies/terms.jsp.

19. Spreitzer, G. M., De Janasz, S. C., & Quinn, R. E. (1999). Empowered to lead: The role of psychological empowerment in leadership. *Journal of Organizational Behavior, 20*(4), 511-526.

20. Houghton, J. D., & Yoho, S. K. (2005). Toward a contingency model of leadership and psychological empowerment: when should self-leadership be encouraged?. *Journal of Leadership & Organizational Studies, 11*(4), 65-83.

21. Ugboro, I. O. (2006). Organizational commitment, job redesign, employee empowerment and intent to quit among survivors of restructuring and downsizing. *Journal of Behavioral and Applied Management, 7*(3), 232-257.

22. Wang, G., & Lee, P. D. (2009). Psychological empowerment and job satisfaction an analysis of interactive effects. *Group & Organization Management, 34*(3), 271-296. DOI 10.1177/1059601108330089.

23. Liao, H., Toya, K., Lepak, D. P., & Hong, Y. (2009). Do they see eye to eye? Management and employee perspectives of high-performance work systems and influence processes on service quality. *Journal of Applied Psychology, 94*(2), 371.

24. Zhang, X., & Bartol, K. M. (2010). Linking empowering leadership and employee creativity: The influence of psychological empowerment, intrinsic motivation, and creative process engagement. *Academy of Management Journal, 53*(1), 107-128.

25.   Rawat, P. S. Effect of Psychological Empowerment on Commitment of Employees: An Empirical Study. *2ⁿᵈ International Conference on Humanities, Historical and social sciences IPEDR*, 17, 143-147.

26.   Thomas, A. Avijan Dutta. (2011). Impact of psychological component on organizational commitment A case study with reference to an Air Conditioning organization in India. *Academy of Management Journal*, *38*, 1442-1465.

27.   Al-Swidi, A. K., Nawawi, M. K. M., & Al-Hosam, A. (2012). Is the Relationship between Employees' Psychological Empowerment and Employees' Job Satisfaction Contingent on the Transformational Leadership? A Study on the Yemeni Islamic Banks. *Asian Social Science, 8*(10), 130-150. URL: http://dx.doi.org/10.5539/ass.v8n10p130.

28.   Dimitriades, Z., & Kufidu, S. (2004). Individual, job, organizational and contextual correlates of employment empowerment: some Greek evidence. *Electronic Journal of Business Ethic and Organization studies*, 9 (2), 36-43.

29.   Mackie, K. S., Holahan, C. K., & Gottlieb, N. H. (2001). Employee involvement management practices, work stress, and depression in employees of a human services residential care facility. *Human Relations, 54*(8), 1065-1092. DOI: 10.1177/0018726701548004.

30.   Chughtai, A. A. (2008). Impact of job involvement on in-role job performance and organizational citizenship behavior. *Journal of Behavioral and Applied Management, 9*(2), 169-183.

31.   Mohsan, F., Nawaz, M. M., & Khan, M. S. (2011). Coaching as a Predictor of Motivation and Job Involvement: Evidence from Banking Sector of Pakistan. *European Journal of Social Sciences, 22*(3), 406-413.

32.   Wood, S., & de Menezes, L. M. (2011). High involvement management, high-performance work systems and well-being. *The International Journal of Human Resource Management, 22*(07), 1586-1610.

33. Ueda, Y. (2011). Organizational citizenship behavior in a Japanese organization: The effects of job involvement, organizational commitment, and collectivism. *Journal of Behavioral Studies in Business, 4*, 1-14.

34. Kirkman, B. L., & Shapiro, D. L. (2001). The impact of cultural values on job satisfaction and organizational commitment in self-managing work teams: The mediating role of employee resistance. *Academy of Management Journal, 44*(3), 557-569.

35. Triandis, H. C. (2006). Cultural intelligence in organizations. *Group & Organization Management, 31*(1), 20-26. DOI 10.1177/1059601105275253

36. Ang, S., Van Dyne, L., & Koh, C. (2006). Personality correlates of the four-factor model of cultural intelligence. *Group & Organization Management, 31*(1), 100-123. DOI: 10.1177/1059601105275267

37. Templer, K. J., Tay, C., & Chandrasekar, N. A. (2006). Motivational cultural intelligence, realistic job preview, realistic living conditions preview, and cross-cultural adjustment. *Group & Organization Management, 31*(1), 154-173. DOI: 10.1177/1059601105275293

38. Ang, S., Van Dyne, L., Koh, C., Ng, K. Y., Templer, K. J., Tay, C., & Chandrasekar, N. A. (2007). Cultural intelligence: Its measurement and effects on cultural judgment and decision making, cultural adaptation and task performance. *Management and Organization Review, 3*(3), 335-371. DOI: 10.1111/j.1740-8784.2007.00082.x

39. Van Dyne, L., Ang, S., & Livermore, D. (2010). Cultural intelligence: A pathway for leading in a rapidly globalizing world. *Leading across differences: Cases and perspectives*, 131-138.

40. Ng, K. Y., Van Dyne, L., & Ang, S. (2009). From experience to experiential learning: Cultural intelligence as a learning capability for global leader development. *Academy of Management Learning & Education, 8*(4), 511-526.

41. Van Dyne, L., & Pierce, J. L. (2004). Psychological ownership and feelings of possession: Three field studies predicting em-

ploye attitudes and organizational citizenship behavior. *Journal of Organizational Behavior, 25*(4), 439-459. Doi: 10.1002/job.249

42.   Mayhew, M. G., Ashkanasy, N. M., Bramble, T., & Gardner, J. (2007). A study of the antecedents and consequences of psychological ownership in organizational settings. *The Journal of social psychology, 147*(5), 477-500. DOI: 10.3200/socp.147.5.477-500.

43.   Reb, J., & Connolly, T. (2010). Possession, Feelings of Ownership, and the Endowment Effect. *Judgment and Decision Making, 2*(2), 107-114.

44.   Avey, J. B., Avolio, B. J., Crossley, C. D., & Luthans, F. (2009). Psychological ownership: Theoretical extensions, measurement and relation to work outcomes. *Journal of Organizational Behavior, 30*(2), 173-191. DOI: 10.1002/job.583

45.   Chung, Y. W., & Moon, H. K. (2011). The moderating effects of collectivistic orientation on psychological ownership and constructive deviant behavior. *International Journal of Business and Management, 6*(12), p65. http://www.ccsenet.org/journal/index.php/ijbm/article/view/10949/9363

46.   Eisenberger, R., Huntington, R., Hutchison S., & Sowa, D. (1986), Perceived Organizational Support. *Journal of Applied Psychology, 71*(3), 500-507.

47.   Eisenberger, R., Fasolo, P., & Davis-LaMastro, V. (1990). Perceived organizational support and employee diligence, commitment, and innovation. *Journal of applied psychology, 75*(1), 51.

48.   Shore, L. M., & Wayne, S. J. (1993). Commitment and employee behavior: comparison of affective commitment and continuance commitment with perceived organizational support. *Journal of Applied Psychology, 78*(5), 774.

49.   Settoon, R. P., Bennett, N., & Liden, R. C. (1996). Social exchange in organizations: Perceived organizational support, leader–member exchange, and employee reciprocity. *Journal of applied psychology, 81*(3), 219.

50. Eisenberger, R., Cummings, J., Armeli, S., & Lynch, P. (1997). Perceived organizational support, discretionary treatment, and job satisfaction. *Journal of Applied Psychology, 82*(5), 812.

51. Armeli, S., Eisenberger, R., Fasolo, P., & Lynch, P. (1998). Perceived organizational support and police performance: the moderating influence of socio emotional needs. *Journal of Applied Psychology, 83*(2), 288. DOI: 10.1037//0021-9010.86.1.42

52. Lynch, P. D., Eisenberger, R., & Armeli, S. (1999). Perceived organizational support: Inferior versus superior performance by wary employees. *Journal of Applied Psychology, 84*(4), 467.

53. Maignan, I., Ferrell, O. C., & Hult, G. T. M. (1999). Corporate citizenship: cultural antecedents and business benefits. *Journal of the Academy of Marketing Science, 27*(4), 455-469.

54. Eisenberger, R., Armeli, S., Rexwinkel, B., Lynch, P. D., & Rhoades, L. (2001). Reciprocation of perceived organizational support. *Journal of applied psychology, 86*(1), 42. DOI: 10.1037//0021-9010.86.1.42

55. Eisenberger, R., Stinglhamber, F., Vandenberghe, C., Sucharski, I. L., & Rhoades, L. (2002). Perceived supervisor support: contributions to perceived organizational support and employee retention. *Journal of Applied Psychology, 87*(3), 565–573. DOI: 10.1037//0021-9010.87.3.565

56. Aselage, J., & Eisenberger, R. (2003). Perceived organizational support and psychological contracts: A theoretical integration. *Journal of Organizational Behavior, 24*(5), 491-509. DOI: 10.1002/job.211

57. Allen, D. G., Shore, L. M., & Griffeth, R. W. (2003). The role of perceived organizational support and supportive human resource practices in the turnover process. *Journal of management, 29*(1), 99-118. http://jom.sagepub.com/cgi/content/abstract/29/1/99

58. Lew, T. Y. (2009). The relationships between perceived organizational support, felt obligation, affective organizational commitment and turnover intention of academics working with private

higher educational institutions in Malaysia. *European Journal of Social Sciences, 9*(1), 72-87.

59. Williams, L. J., & Anderson, S. E. (1991). Job satisfaction and organizational commitment as predictors of organizational citizenship and in-role behaviors. *Journal of management, 17*(3), 601-617.

60. Werner, J. M. (1994). Dimensions that make a difference: Examining the impact of in-role and extra role behaviors on supervisory ratings. *Journal of Applied Psychology, 79*(1), 98.

61. Diefendorff, J. M., Brown, D. J., Kamin, A. M., & Lord, R. G. (2002). Examining the roles of job involvement and work centrality in predicting organizational citizenship behaviors and job performance. *Journal of Organizational Behavior, 23*(1), 93-108. DOI: 10.1002/job.123

62. Turnley, W. H., Bolino, M. C., Lester, S. W., & Bloodgood, J. M. (2003). The impact of psychological contract fulfillment on the performance of in-role and organizational citizenship behaviors. *Journal of management, 29*(2), 187-206. http://faculty-staff.ou.edu/B/Mark.C.Bolino-1/JOM%202003.B.pdf

63. Vandaele, D., & Gemmel, P. (2006). Performance implications of in-role and extra-role behavior of frontline service employees (No. 06/411). Ghent University, Faculty of Economics and Business Administration.

64. Colquitt, J. A., Scott, B. A., & LePine, J. A. (2007). Trust, trustworthiness, and trust propensity: a meta-analytic test of their unique relationships with risk taking and job performance. *Journal of applied psychology, 92*(4), 909. DOI: 10.1037/0021-9010.92.4.909

65. Christensen, R.K., & Whiting S.W. (2009). The Role of Task Performance and Organizational Citizenship Behavior in Performance Appraisals across Sectors: Exploring the Role of Public Service Motivation. *International Public Service Motivation Research Conference, 7*(9), 1-18.

66.   Judge, T. A., Thoresen, C. J., Bono, J. E., & Patton, G. K. (2001). The job satisfaction–job performance relationship: A qualitative and quantitative review. *Psychological bulletin, 127*(3), 376. DOI: I0.1037//0033-2909.I27.3.376

67.   Huang, C. C., & You, C. S. (2011). The three components of organizational commitment on in-role behaviors and organizational citizenship behaviors. *African Journal of Business Management, 5*(28), 11335-11344. Available online at http://www.academic-journals.org/AJBM DOI: 10.5897/AJBM10.1623

68.   Warr, P., Cook, J., & Wall, T. (1979). Scales for the measurement of some work attitudes and aspects of psychological well being. *Journal of occupational Psychology, 52*(2), 129-148.

69.   Repetti, R. L. (1987). Individual and common components of the social environment at work and psychological well-being. *Journal of Personality and Social Psychology, 52*(4), 710.

70.   Warr, P. (1990). The measurement of well being and other aspects of mental health. Journal of occupational Psychology, 63(3), 193-210.

71.   Parker, S. K., Chmiel, N., & Wall, T. D. (1997). Work characteristics and employee well-being within a context of strategic downsizing. *Journal of occupational health psychology, 2*(4), 289.

72.   De Jonge, J., & Schaufeli, W. B. (1998). Job characteristics and employee well-being: A test of Warr's Vitamin Model in health care workers using structural equation modeling. *Journal of Organizational Behavior, 19*(4), 387-407.

73.   Jonge, J., Dormann, C., Janssen, P. P., Dollard, M. F., Landeweerd, J. A., & Nijhuis, F. J. (2001). Testing reciprocal relationships between job characteristics and psychological well being: A cross lagged structural equation model. *Journal of Occupational and organizational Psychology, 74*(1), 29-46.

74.   Harter, J. K., Schmidt, F. L., & Keyes, C. L. (2003). Well-being in the workplace and its relationship to business outcomes: A review of the Gallup studies. *Flourishing: Positive psychology and the life well-lived*, 2, 205-224.

75.   McKee-Ryan, F., Song, Z., Wanberg, C. R., & Kinicki, A. J. (2005). Psychological and physical well-being during unemployment: a meta-analytic study. *Journal of Applied Psychology, 90*(1), 53. DOI: 10.1037/0021-9010.90.1.53

76.   Panaccio, A., & Vandenberghe, C. (2009). Perceived organizational support, organizational commitment and psychological well-being: A longitudinal study. *Journal of Vocational Behavior, 75*(2), 224-236. DOI: 10.1016/j.jvb.2009.06.002

77.   Robertson, I. T., & Cooper, C. L. (2010). Full engagement: the integration of employee engagement and psychological well-being. *Leadership & Organization Development Journal, 31*(4), 324-336. DOI: 10.1108/01437731011043348

78.   Avey, J. B., Luthans, F., Smith, R. M., & Palmer, N. F. (2010). Impact of positive psychological capital on employee well-being over time. *Journal of occupational health psychology, 15*(1), 17. DOI: 10.1037/a001699. http://digitalcommons.unl.edu/cgi/viewcontent.cgi?article=1055&context=managementfacpub

79.   Böckerman, P., Ilmakunnas, P., & Johansson, E. (2011). Job security and employee well-being: Evidence from matched survey and register data. *Labour Economics, 18*(4), 547-554.

80.   Meyer, J. P., Allen, N. J., & Smith, C. A. (1993). Commitment to organizations and occupations: Extension and test of a three-component conceptualization. *Journal of applied psychology, 78*(4), 538.

81.   Moynihan, L. M., Boswell, W. R., & Boudreau, J. W. (2000). The influence of job satisfaction and organizational commitment on executive withdrawal and performance. *Center for Advanced Human Resource Studies* CAHRS Working Paper Series. Paper 94. http://digitalcommons.ilr.cornell.edu/cahrswp/94.

82.   Meyer, J. P., Stanley, D. J., Herscovitch, L., & Topolnytsky, L. (2002). Affective, continuance, and normative commitment to the organization: A meta-analysis of antecedents, correlates, and consequences. *Journal of vocational behavior, 61*(1), 20-52. doi:10.1006/jvbe.2001.1842

83. Baruch, Y., & Winkelmann–Gleed, A. (2002). Multiple commitments: A conceptual framework and empirical investigation in a community health service trust. *British Journal of Management, 13*(4), 337-357.

84. Babakus, E., Yavas, U., Karatepe, O. M., & Avci, T. (2003). The effect of management commitment to service quality on employees' affective and performance outcomes. *Journal of the Academy of Marketing Science, 31*(3), 272-286. DOI: 10.1177/0092070303253525

85. Ito, J. K., & Brotheridge, C. M. (2005). Does supporting employees' career adaptability lead to commitment, turnover, or both?. *Human Resource Management, 44*(1), 5-19. DOI: 10.1002/hrm.20037

86. Çelik, C. (2008). Relationship of organizational commitment and job satisfaction: a field study of tax office employees. *International Conference on Management and Economics (ICME)*, 138-155. http://ces.epoka.edu.al/icme/11.pdf

87. Uygur, A., & Kilic, G. (2009). A Study into Organizational Commitment and Job Involvement: An Application Towards the Personnel in the Central Organization for Ministry of Health in Turkey. *Ozean journal of applied sciences, 2*(1), 113-125.

88. Kim, H. J., Tavitiyaman, P., & Kim, W. G. (2009). The effect of management commitment to service on employee service behaviors: The mediating role of job satisfaction. *Journal of Hospitality & Tourism Research, 33*(3), 369-390. DOI: 10.1177/1096348009338530

89. Kuean, W. L., Kaur, S., & Wong, E. S. K. (2010). Intention to Quit: The Malaysian Companies Perspectives. *Journal of Applied Sciences, 10*(19), 2251-2260.

90. Liu, Y., & Cohen, A. (2010). Values, commitment, and OCB among Chinese employees. *International Journal of Intercultural Relations, 34*(5), 493-506.

91. Shah, N., & Shah, S. G. S. (2010). Relationships between employee readiness for organisational change, supervisor and peer

relations and demography. *Journal of Enterprise Information Management, 23*(5), 640-652. DOI 10.1108/17410391011083074, www.emeraldinsight.com/1741-0398.htm

92.   Abdullah., (2011). Evaluation of Allen and Meyer's Organizational Commitment Scale: A Cross-Cultural Application in Pakistan. *Journal of Education and Vocational Research, 1*(3), 80-86.

93.   Moorman, R. H., Niehoff, B. P., & Organ, D. W. (1993). Treating employees fairly and organizational citizenship behavior: Sorting the effects of job satisfaction, organizational commitment, and procedural justice. *Employee Responsibilities and Rights Journal, 6*(3), 209-225.

94.   Allison, B.J., Voss R.S., & Huston C. R., (2001). An Empirical Investigation of the Impact of SDB on the Relationship between OCB and Individual Performance. http://www.sbaer.uca.edu/Research/acme/2001/38.pdf

95.   Cardona, P., & Espejo, A. (2002). Effect of the Rating Source in Organizational Citizenship Behavior: A Multitrait-multimethod Analysis. *IESE Working Paper No D/474-E.* Available at SSRN: http://ssrn.com/abstract=443438 or http://dx.doi.org/10.2139/ssrn.443438

96.   Farh, J. L., Zhong, C. B., & Organ, D. W. (2004). Organizational citizenship behavior in the People's Republic of China. *Organization Science, 15*(2), 241-253. DOI: 10.1287/1030.0051

97.   Emmerik, I. H. V., Jawahar, I. M., & Stone, T. H. (2005). Associations among altruism, burnout dimensions, and organizational citizenship behavior. *Work & Stress*, 19(1), 93-100. DOI: 10.1080/02678370500046283

98.   Podsakoff, N. P., Whiting, S. W., Podsakoff, P. M., & Blume, B. D. (2009). Individual-and organizational-level consequences of organizational citizenship behaviors: A meta-analysis. *Journal of Applied Psychology, 94*(1), 122. DOI:10.1037/a0013079

99.   Farzianpour, F., Foroushani, A. R., Kamjoo, H., & Hosseini, S. S. (2011). Organizational Citizenship Behavior (OCB) among the

Managers of Teaching Hospitals. *American Journal of Economics and Business Administration, 3* (3), 534-542.

100. Ehtiyar, V. R., Aktas Alan, A., & Oemueris, E. (2010). The role of organizational citizenship behavior on university student's academic success. *Tourism and Hospitality Management, 16*(1), 47-61.

101. Mohsan F et al., (2011). Impact of Job Involvement on Organizational Citizenship Behavior (OCB) and In-Role Job Performance: A Study on Banking Sector of Pakistan. *European Journal of Social Sciences, 24*(4), 494-502.

102. Chester I. Barnard, The Functions of the Executive, Introduction by Kenneth R. Andrews, 30th Anniversary Edition, 2002 printing, Harvard University press, pp 82-90

103. James G. March and Herbert A. Simon , Organizations, John wiley & Sons, Inc. 9th Printing 1967, pp 84

104. Psychological Contract Inventory Technical Report Denise M. Rousseau, Version 2: February 2000

105. Spreitzer, Gretchen M. (1995), Psychological empowerment in the workplace: Dimensions, measurement, and validation. *Academy of Management Journal, 38*(5): 1442-1465.

106. Lawler, E. E. (1988), Transformation from control to involvement In R. H. Kilman, T. J. Covin and Associates (eds.), corporate transformation (pp. 46-65). San Francisco: Jossey-Bass.

107. Lawler,E.(1986), High Involvement Management San Francisco: Jossey-Bass. http://www.eric.ed.gov/ERICWebPortal/search/detailmini.jsp?_nfpb=true&_&ERICExtSearch_SearchValue_0=ED314989&ERICExtSearch_SearchType_0=no&accno=ED314989

108. Ang, S., & Van Dyne, L. (2008), Handbook on cultural intelligence: Theory, measurement and applications. Armonk, NY: M.E. Sharpe.

109. Linn van dyne and Jon L. Pierce, (2004), Psychological ownership and feelings of possession: three field studies predicting

employee attitudes and organizational citizenship behavior, *Journal of Organizational Behavior*, Vol.25, pp 439–459

110.   Stephen Armeli, Robert Eisenberger, Peter Fasolo, and Patrick Lynch (1998), Perceived Organizational Support and Police Performance The Moderating Influence of Socio emotional Needs, *Journal of Applied Psychology*, Vol. 83 (2), pp 288-297

111.   Larry J. Williams and Stella E. Anderson, (1991), Job satisfaction and Organizational Commitment as a predictor of Organizational citizenship and In role behavior, *Journal of Management*, Vol.17(3), pp 601-617.

112.   Peter Warr, John Cook and Toby Wall, (1979), Scales for the measurement of some work attitudes and aspects of psychological well-being, *Journal of Occupational Psychology*, Vol.52, pp 129-148.

113.   John P. Meyer, David J. Stanley, Lynne Herscovitch, and Laryssa Topolnytsky, (2002), Affective, Continuance, and Normative Commitment to the Organization: A Meta-analysis of Antecedents, Correlates, and Consequences, *Journal of Vocational Behavior*, Vol. 61,pp 20–52. doi:10.1006/jvbe.2001.1842.

114.   Philip M. Podsakoff, Scott B. MacKenzie, Robert H. Moorman & Richard Fetter (1990), Transformational Leader Behaviors and Their Effects on Followers' Trust in Leader, Satisfaction, and Organizational Citizenship Behaviors, Leadership Quarterly, Vol. l(2), pp 107-142.

REFERENCES

1. Andrew Clark and Fabien Postel-Vinay, February 2005, Job Security and Job Protection, IZA Discussion Paper No. 1489.

2. Bakan, ., Büyükbee, T., & Erahan, B. (2011). An Investigation of Organizational Commitment and Education Level among Employees. *Int. J. Emerg. Sci*, *1*(3), 231-245.

3. Bandura, A. (1977). Self-efficacy: toward a unifying theory of behavioral change. *Psychological review*, *84*(2), 191.

4. Barling, J. & Cooper, C. (2008). Handbook of Organizational Behavior, Sage. 17-34.

5. Becker, H. S. (1960). Notes on the concept of commitment. *American journal of Sociology*, 66 (1), 32-40.

6. Cleveland, J. N., & Shore, L. M. (1992). Self-and supervisory perspectives on age and work attitudes and performance. *Journal of Applied Psychology*, *77*(4), 469.

7. Conger, J. A., & Kanungo, R. N. (1988). The empowerment process: Integrating theory and practice. *Academy of management review*, *13*(3), 471-482.

8. Cooper, D. R., & Schindler, P. S. (2003). Business research methods. Special Indian Edition 9th edition, Tata McGraw-Hill Edition 2006, ISBN-13: 978-0-07-062019-3, ISBN-10: 0-07-062019-9.

9. Cuthill, M. (2002). Exploratory research: citizen participation, local government and sustainable development in Australia. *Sustainable Development*, *10*(2), 79-89.

10. Emerson, R. M. (1962). Power-dependence relations. *American sociological review*, 31-41. Jay, R. (2001). *Fast thinking manager's manual*. ISBN 0-273-65298-2.

11. Gouldner, A. W. (1960). The norm of reciprocity: A preliminary statement. *American sociological review*, 161-178.

12. Hooper, D., Coughlan, J., & Mullen, M. (2008). Structural equation modeling: guidelines for determining model fit. *Articles*, 2. www.ejbrm.com/issue/download.html?idArticle=183.

13. Kidder, D. L. (2002). The influence of gender on the performance of organizational citizenship behaviors. *Journal of Management*, *28*(5), 629-648.

14. Konovsky, M. A., & Pugh, S. D. (1994). Citizenship behavior and social exchange. *Academy of management journal*, *37*(3), 656-669.

15. Kothari, C.R. (1985). Research Methodology- Methods and Techniques, New Delhi, Wiley Eastern Limited.

16. Krohn, M. D., & Massey, J. L. (1980). Social control and delinquent behavior: An examination of the elements of the social bond. *The Sociological Quarterly,21*(4), 529-543.

17. Maryana Sakovska, (2012), Importance of Employee Engagement in Business Environment: Measuring the engagement level of administrative personnel in VUC Aarhus and detecting factors requiring improvement.

18. Meyer, J. P., & Allen, N. J. (1991). A three-component conceptualization of organizational commitment. *Human resource management review*, *1*(1), 61-89.

19. Michael Josephson, DECEMBER 15, 2010 Responsibilities in the Employer-Employee Relationship at JOSEPHSON INSTITUTE

20. Mohrman, S. A., Lawler, E. E., & Mohrman, A. M. (1992). Applying employee involvement in schools. *Educational Evaluation and Policy Analysis*, *14*(4), 347-360. http://ceo.usc.edu/pdf/g91_15.pdf

21. Professor Chris Rowley and Dr Irene Poon, (2009), The Importance for Managers and Organizations of Cultural Intelligence, Centre for Research on Asian Management Cass Knowledge.

22. Qureshi, M. I., Saleem, M. A., & Basheer, S. (2012). Assessment of selected factors on organizational commitment. *Gomal University Journal of Research, 28*, 2.

23. Rosa, P., Carter, S., & Hamilton, D. (1996). Gender as a determinant of small business performance: insights from a British study. *Small Business Economics, 8*(6), 463-478.

24. Rowlinson, M., & Procter, S. (1997). Efficiency and power: organizational economics meets organization theory. *British Journal of Management, 8*(s1), 31-42.

25. Salladarré, F., Hlaimi, B., & Wolff, F. C. (2011). How important is security in the choice of employment? Evidence from European countries. *Economic and Industrial Democracy, 32*(4), 549-567. DOI: 10.1177/0143831X10387649.

26. Taylor, P. J., Catalano, G., & Walker, D. R. (2002). Exploratory analysis of the world city network. *Urban Studies, 39*(13), 2377-2394.

27. The Importance of Obtaining Job Security by Frances Burks, eHow Contributor Dasgupta, S. (2001). *Employment security: conceptual and statistical issues* (Vol. 10). International Labour Office. Geneva, April ISBN 92-2-112450-9.

28. The Importance of Obtaining Job Security by Ralph Heibutzki, Demand Media.

29. The Times 100 Business case studies, Rights and responsibilities of employers and employees

30. Waldman, D. A., & Avolio, B. J. (1986). A meta-analysis of age differences in job performance. *Journal of Applied Psychology, 71*(1), 33.

WEBSITES

- http://www.cs.uu.nl/docs/vakken/arm/SPSS/spss7.pdf

- http://www.agbioforum.org/v14n1/v14n1a03-annunziata.htm

- http://www.ifrnd.org/JSDS/1(3)%20Apr%202011/Analyzing%20the%20Risk%20Factors%20of_Supply%20Chain%20Management.pdf

- http://www.docstoc.com/docs/47573905/Chapter-7---Factor-Analysis---SPSS

- http://thinkingbookworm.typepad.com/blog/2012/04/the-effect-of-country-of-origin-on-products-hypothesis-and-analysis.html

- http://www.docstoc.com/docs/79675729/FMCG-HUL-premix

- http://www.nscb.gov.ph/events/mdg/papers/october%201/session%202/Sri%20Lanka_session%202.ppt

- http://www.academia.edu/696822/impact_of_IT_on_customer_expectation_in_academic_libraries

- http://www.iiste.org/Journals/index.php/IEL/article/download/2237/2250

- http://www.scribd.com/doc/45247936/Final-Report

- http://www.scribd.com/doc/139527188/Factor-Analysis

- http://www.scribd.com/doc/37502401/A-Project-Report

- http://publib.boulder.ibm.com/infocenter/spssstat/v20r0m0/topic/com.ibm.spss.statistics.cs/fac_cars_communalities_01.htm

- https://experts.missouristate.edu/display/csvhelpdesk/Statistical+Analysis+-+Dimension+Reduction+-+Factor+Analysis

- http://gsgl.shufe.edu.cn/jswz/web/67/soft/200641316173626902.doc

- http://eisenberger.psych.udel.edu/POS.html

INDEX

Public sector 6, 7, 11, 12, 14, 41, 48,
  67, 79, 81, 83, 84, 86, 91, 92,
  93, 94, 95, 96, 97, 98, 99, 100,
  101, 102, 103, 104, 105, 106,
  109, 110, 111, 113, 117, 121,
  129, 137, 139, 140, 166, 169,
  170, 171, 172, 173, 176, 182,
  184, 187, 188, 189, 190, 192
Public sector bank 6, 7, 48, 67, 79,
  81, 83, 84, 86, 91, 92, 93, 94,
  95, 96, 97, 98, 99, 100, 101,
  102, 103, 104, 105, 106, 109,
  110, 111, 113, 117, 121, 129,
  137, 139, 140, 166, 169, 170,
  171, 172, 173, 176, 182, 184,
  187, 188, 189, 190, 192
Pullay et al 30

Q

Quinn 16, 62, 199

R

Rawat 18, 200
Reb 24, 202
Regression analysis 7, 14, 18, 22, 38
Reichers, 1985 63
Reliability analysis 7, 86
Repetti 34, 205
Retail sales employees 28
Rexwinkel 28, 203
Rhoades 28, 57, 58, 203
Rhoades & Eisenberger, 2002 57
R.M. Emerson 1962 52
Robertson 36, 206
Roehling 9, 197
Rosen 15, 199
Rousseau 12, 49, 179, 198, 209
Rousseau, 1989 49
Rousseau & Tijoriwala, 1998 49

S

Sample't' test 7
Schaufeli 35, 205

Schmidt 35, 55, 205
Schmidt and Hunter's (2000) 55
Scott 31, 204, 210
Self efficacy Theory (1986) 52
Settoon 26, 202
Shah and Shah (2010) 41
Shapico 21
Shore 9, 14, 26, 29, 57, 58, 121, 197,
  198, 202, 203, 211
Shore (1992) 121
Shore and Tetrick 9
Shore & Shore, 1995 57, 58
Singapore 22
Smith 37, 62, 65, 206
Social Exchange Theory 63
Social Exchange Theory Blau (1964)
  49
Song 36, 206
Sowa 25, 57, 202
Sowa, 1986 57
Spector, 1986 53
Spreitzer 14, 15, 16, 179, 199, 209
Stanley 38, 206, 210
Sternberg 55
Sternberg et al., 2000 55
Stinglhamber 28, 203
Stone (2005) 43
Sucharshki 28
Sutton 13, 198

T

Tavitiyaman 40, 207
Tax Office employees 39
Tay 22, 201
Team commitment 15
Team culture 2
Templer 22, 201
Thailand 40
Thoits 58
Thoits, 1992 58
Thomas 15, 18, 53, 200
Thomas & Velthouse, 1990 53
Thoresen 32, 205
Thorndike and Stein, 1937 55